CITIZEN CAN

JUST A CONCERN PERSON WHO BELIEVES WE CAN

ATTAIN A HIGHER LEVEL OF MUTUAL EXISTENCE

By

John L. Hurlbut

ISBN: 979-8-8691-6277-9

Printed in the United States of America

Published by Book Writing Pioneer

www.bookwritingpioneer.com

TABLE OF CONTENTS

ACKNOWLEDGMENTS

I have a lifetime of people (thousands) who I have met who contributed to this book in one way or another. I am grateful to all of these citizens for contributing to my life journey toward good citizenship. These included my early family (my grandmother, grandfather, several uncles, my stepfather, and my mother) and my own created family, which includes my wife (Nena), children (Greg and Kathy), and grandchildren (Ryan and Ethan). I also want to give special thanks to my wife's family (her deceased parents, Gavino and Esther Unchuan), Pacquito, Marissa, Melissa, Anya, and Jonathan. I learned so much from my time with them.

I want to include my classmates, co-workers, business associates, military buddies, kids whom I served, and senior citizens who I have had the pleasure to meet and serve. I would also like to thank the many people and causes I initially or permanently disagreed with. These, too, contributed to my journey that challenged my thinking and, in some cases, provided me with a new productive course to follow.

It is impossible to name all the citizens who have positively impacted my life. However, I need to name a few in addition to the members of my direct family and my wife's family who stand out.

My grandmother, Mama Kitty, and Uncle Jack provided me with the childhood moral foundation that allowed me to evolve.

My mother (Dorothy) and stepfather (Herbert) added to my adult value system that equipped me further in my journey toward good citizenship.

During my adult journey, some special people have impacted me in a way that has kept me on the course toward better citizenship. They are Frank Disanto, Paul Terlemezian, Melissa Wade, as well as Lee and Liz Durham.

Finally, a very special thanks goes to Maribel Dionisio and Lissa Moran. This book would not have been finished without Maribel's encouragement and Lissa's willingness to be my editor.

PREFACE

Auguste Rodin's *The Thinker* says it all. This renowned sculpture captures the essence of what I convey in this book. The figure's nakedness represents the universality of human nature, a man in his purest form—honest, raw, exposed. Caught in a moment of deep pondering, the subject appears at rest but exudes a quiet power. The power of reasoning, analyzing, questioning, learning, and creating—all of which I am calling us all to do as citizens of America and of the world.

Amidst a maelstrom of personal, national, and global crises, I urge us all to pause. Take honest stock of the situation—as I sought to do in this book. Draw upon our inner strength, courage, and faith to think independently, stand up for what we know deep in our hearts is right, and face life's challenges with hope and resolve.

THAT MAY JUST WORK.

INTRODUCTION

Before anyone reads this book, I want to issue a warning. I am not an expert in anything. I am not Mensa qualified. Instead, I have been self-destructive at times in my life. I have had racist thoughts in the past and questioned God. Therefore, there may be many reasons not to follow my ideas on good citizenship.

With the warning expressed, I would like to share how you may benefit from my journey toward good citizenship.

I turned 76 years old on October 1, 2023. During those years, I have made many mistakes. However, during my life, many people impacted me in a way that allowed me to turn the pages of my bad behavior and create new pages of better behavior. Those experiences have provided me with wisdom that I now feel qualified to disseminate to others, including my family and friends.

In this book, you will see some of the good, bad, and ugly experiences in my life. I am grateful for all of them. Some were painful, and it took me a while to understand what I could learn from them. But some were awesome and provided me with a sense of purpose. As a result of all of these experiences, along with the eventual positive manner in which I processed them, I now feel free. Obviously, I am not perfect. However, I feel that I am now wise enough to recognize when I have stinking thoughts and am going down the wrong path and when I am following good citizenship qualities.

This book is not so much about me. It is about the many people who feel lost, with no purpose, and powerless to make a difference. Hopefully, the citizenship tools expressed herein will give the readers the impetus to make positive changes in their lives, where necessary, and to try, however small it seems, to make a difference in their own family, the community, and/or the world at large. Take my word, it is possible. Something small may result in something big.

In this book, I used the United States of America as the main target to benefit from good citizenship. However, if it works for the USA, it may very well work for the world at large.

I start by defining who we are as citizens of the United States of America and what the USA stands for. I then outline my ideas of the elements required of a good citizen. To emphasize the importance of good citizenship, I share quotes on citizenship from each of our US Presidents.

After presenting some of my life experiences, I describe my idea of the major roadblocks to becoming a good citizen.

As I continue, I list some of the significant problems we are encountering in the 21st century and the characteristics necessary for a good citizen to tackle them.

I hope that Mama Kitty (my grandmother) and Uncle Jack (my early father figure) will be happy with me for presenting my ideas to you. Through their guidance, I learned the two most important values I express constantly in this book. They are ***LOVE*** and ***THE GOLDEN RULE.***

CHAPTER ONE

Who Are We?

The United States of America has arguably been the longest-lasting experiment as a democratic republic in the history of the world. In its almost 250 years of development, certain events have defined America to create and sustain its existence. I believe the most significant were the Revolutionary War, the War of 1812, the United States Civil War, the Spanish-American War, World War I, World War II, the Vietnam War, and the war on terrorism, as we know it today.

In its first 200 years, America sacrificed more than 1.3 million brave soldiers to defend its experiment of freedom, support other nations who desire the same, and further define itself as a free republic. Documents and speeches created by wise leaders who divinely appeared at critical times during our development influenced the bravery of these patriots. In his book "Give Me Liberty,: Richard Brookhiser presented his perspective on the most crucial among these:

1) *Minutes of the Jamestown General Assembly defined the rules by which we self-govern.*

2) *The Flushing Remonstrance laid the foundation for freedom of religion.*

3) *The Trial of John Peter Zenger provided us with freedom of speech.*

4) *The Declaration of Independence cited that our Creator gave us certain inalienable rights, including life, liberty, and the pursuit of happiness.*

5) *The Manumission Society Constitution made significant strides in liberating enslaved people.*

6) *The Constitution of the United States defines how our federal government is to operate, distinguishes between Federal and State powers, and protects various individual liberties of free citizens.*

7) *The Seneca Falls Declaration called for voting rights for women.*

8) *The Gettysburg Address provided a eulogy to our fallen soldiers and stated that "we are better than this" while embracing the Declaration of Independence and the Constitution.*

9) *The New Colossus welcomed the world to take part in our liberty. However, the Statue of Liberty did challenge those who liked to participate. As Brookhiser paraphrases, "Come here, be like us; I will show you the way."*

10) *The Cross of Gold Speech further defined us as a nation with economic equality.*

11) *The Monroe Doctrine further explained that the Western Hemisphere represents freedom from individual leaders, and there should be no kings here.*

12) *The Arsenal of Democracy Fireside Chat made an impression on the free world that Nazism is evil and Britain should be free of it.*

13) *The 'Tear Down That Wall' speech sought to eliminate Communists as a ruling class in Europe.*

Brookhiser's list of events spans 377 years, three of them occurring in the 166 years before our Declaration of Independence. However, like our Constitution, which allows Amendments to update the Federal rules necessary for providing its citizens the civil liberties expected in a free society as the nation matures, all the events and speeches mentioned above are pertinent to their times.

To effectively act as a free society with a strong foundation of liberty, studying and understanding defining historical events such as those referred to above is necessary. But we still haven't determined who the citizens of America, and subsequently, the United States of America, are. To do that, we need to do a deep dive into the various components of our culture. Too often today, we are defined as Republican or Democrat, conservative or liberal, male or female, black or white, rich or poor, to mention only a few. Americans are much more than that. It is crucial to respect our culture or roots (so to speak), which help define who we are as individuals. However, placing us into broader designated groups has an inherent risk of *"group think"* that, if taken too far without respect for the rights of other groups of citizens, can lead to destructive unintended *(or more disastrous)* intended consequences.

Today, we are a complex society. The United States of America consists of many ethnic groups. A much-overlooked example of this fact is that we have over 550 Native American Tribes in the United States. The largest are the Navajo, Cherokee, and Sioux. The Native American population totals over 6.5 million, or 2% of the people in the U.S.

Today, our demographics are more popularly described *(to mention only a few categories)* as white, black, Asian, European, Mexican, Middle Eastern, or sometimes Christian *(with its many denominations)*, Jewish, follower of Islam, Buddhist, Hindu, etc. But, again, these do not define who we are as Americans. We need to look deeper into our history to help ourselves here.

America's colonization, starting in Jamestown in 1606 and continuing to 1898, primarily involved five countries *(England, Holland, France, Scotland, and Spain)*. Germany and Italy made failed attempts during this time; however, their influence was felt more after the 19th century. From 1619 to 1865, an estimated 600,000 enslaved people were imported directly or indirectly from Africa to the 13 original American colonies and the seven additional states admitted by 1865. In addition, Native Americans have inhabited America for over 15,000 years, creating another level of complexity for safe relations. Before the Declaration of Independence, America underwent 166 painful years of integrating its various cultures.

Finally, American settlers banded together to resist and rebel against the tyranny of the countries responsible for colonizing America. Over time, a new nation emerged: The United States of America. The creation of New America brought with it new challenges for the settlers. They had to manage the consequences of refusing to follow the burdensome laws of their *"leaders"* from the other side of the Atlantic Ocean. Still, they also had to learn to self-regulate and to find a way to integrate all their national and religious differences. They subsequently found that delaying solutions to the scourge of slavery and unjust Native American treatment would complicate the development of this new experiment in liberty.

In my thoughts and observation of the struggles and successes of America's first 417 years of multicultural existence, I define our great country in three stages:

- Early Development (1607-1776)

- Formal Development (1776-1865)

- Maturity and Destiny (1865 to the present)

During the Early Development stage, Americans learned that there was a need for all its old and new cultures to work together effectively. Here, they defined the processes by which they governed and protected themselves and established the rules necessary to maintain their freedoms, including their methods of worship and the exercise of free speech.

The Formal Development stage first gave us three vital documents defining America's colonies *(and subsequently states)* as the United States of America. Its Bill of Rights, The Declaration of Independence, and the Constitution of the United States gave its citizens identity and an exemplary structure within which to operate as a free society that would provide these citizens hope for the future. But unfortunately, it took 87 years of this stage to rid this developing nation of slavery, a cancer that stayed with us until the Emancipation Proclamation of 1863.

The Maturity and Destiny stage further defined our inclusiveness by providing women and Native Americans the right to vote. Then, with great difficulty, we assimilated newly freed slaves and other African Americans into our sacred structure, culminating with The Civil Rights Act of 1964. Finally, the Maturity and Destiny stage further defined the United States as a beacon of liberty for the rest of the world. It established rules regarding our need to protect the freedom of other nations from oppression. This focus on the sovereignty of other countries was evident as we entered the world scene to fight against the Nazis, extract the free world from communism, and stop Japan from trying to dominate all of Southeast Asia.

So, what does it mean to be an American? In other words, ***Who Are We?*** I see each citizen as cells or building blocks of our divinely created structure, The United States of America. Each cell is uniquely different and requires the ability to be free and robust to benefit the divine network within which it operates. Like our citizens, our cells have many unique parts in their structure. After centuries of developing relationships with other cultures, they have created a new culture of diversity, even within a given cell. Many of us today seek to define our roots through DNA tests.

This idea that we are unique and essential cells within ourselves should be enough to qualify us for the opportunity to be free to define our views of life, liberty, and the pursuit of happiness. To do this, we must fulfill our role as law-abiding citizens who love and protect our family unit, extend that love and protection to our neighbors, and treat all others as we would have them treat us.

In summary, it would be shortsighted to define oneself or anyone else by broad buckets, such as race, gender, sexual orientation, or the magnitude of their wealth. To reach this great country's full potential,

America's citizens are responsible for feeding it with the elements necessary for effective and sustained growth. This activity may require the citizens to look deeper into their friends, neutral acquaintances, even those they define as enemies or segments of society that they deem challenging to reach to better define them with the goal of inclusion, not separation. We must cultivate diversity of thought and use it to help us grow. Proper education, a commitment to lifetime learning, and a dedication to something greater than oneself are powerful tools to address this.

We cannot sustain the success of this great country without educating the rest of the world, friends or foes, about who we are and why we exist. But first, we need to strengthen ourselves. Unless we continually educate ourselves and the rest of the world that the heart and soul of The United States of America is liberty and act accordingly, we will not be able to know Who We Are.

The following Preamble to our Constitution best outlines Who We Are: "We, the People of the United States, in Order to form a more perfect Union, *establish Justice, insure domestic Tranquility, provide for the common defense, promote the general Welfare, and secure the Blessings of Liberty to ourselves and our Posterity*, do ordain and establish this Constitution for the United States of America."

CHAPTER TWO

Every Citizen's Responsibility

As I cited in Chapter 1, I see each American citizen as a cell or building block of America's *(and, by example, the rest of the world's)* divinely created structure. Please understand that I am not a scientist or, for that matter, a historian or even an experienced writer. I am a concerned citizen of this great country with a wife, children, grandchildren, and other relatives and friends who I want to be free to pursue happiness and understand that they are responsible for their actions. Moreover, their efforts impact other citizens either directly or indirectly. With this as a caveat, let's explore my premise that we citizens are analogous to human body cells.

According to the National Library of Medicine: "Cells are the basic building blocks of all living things. The human body is composed of trillions of cells. They provide structure for the body, take in nutrients from food, convert them into energy, and carry out specialized functions. Cells also contain the body's hereditary material and can make copies of themselves." In addition, "Cells have many parts, each with a different function. Some of these parts, called organelles, are specialized structures that perform certain tasks within the cell."

How does this definition of cells correlate to American citizens' activities, importance, and responsibility? First, there are approximately 340 million people *(in my words, citizens)* in the United States and close to 8 billion worldwide. These numbers are far from the "trillions" that describe the number of cells in the human body but are large enough to illustrate how impaired functions of either body cells or citizen cells can harm all.

Second, cells provide structure to the body. As I will discuss further later, citizens have a similar responsibility to create and implement while reviewing and amending the social norms they establish. The ultimate structure created by our citizens must have the opportunity to benefit all citizens. As I will elaborate later, no system is perfect, and some citizens may operate outside the established norm for specific reasons. Examples may be situations unique to the citizen or his/her family, a structure that is outdated and requires amending or possibly a citizen's choice to operate under his or her own set of rules. Each situation requires attention that is unique to the problem.

I want to stress that the goal is not to create citizen clones. The goal is to create a system whereby all citizens can freely pursue their personal goals and be happy while fulfilling their responsibilities to themselves, their families, and the community (local, national, and global). We are all unique individuals created by God who should be expected to live in a world created by God in a way God would approve. Examples would be to **LOVE** all and **DO UNTO OTHERS AS YOU WOULD HAVE THEM DO UNTO YOU.**

Third, cells take in nutrients, convert those nutrients into energy, and carry out specific functions. This process is not unlike the citizens' responsibility to take care of themselves (physically, mentally, and spiritually) to create the individual energy and knowledge necessary to thrive and be helpful to themselves and others.

Fourth, as human beings like human body cells, we are unique. This uniqueness is one of the fundamental reasons we are helpful in society. Earlier, I mentioned organelles-specialized structures that perform specific tasks within the cell. Citizens also have similarly specialized functions. Some are internal, such as those in organs vital to the human body's activities, growth, and longevity. These functions require a positive relationship between citizens and healthcare professionals to maximize effectiveness. Other organelle-like functions that the citizen cell has at its disposal are the following: Use of knowledge, the ability to learn, access to methods of brain development, and multiple ways to acquire capabilities for physical, spiritual, and mental growth. All of these are integral parts of a structure that can improve a citizen's quality of life while preparing him or her to be a vital part of the healthy growth of the community.

A couple of hundred cell types group the trillions of cells in the human body. These types place the cells into important categories designed to streamline the activities of the human body. Each cell type has a specific function, and most often, these cells form tissues, which combine and create unique organs. The resultant organs put every kind of cell into action, where every cell knows its purpose.

All human beings are required to work effectively together to create mutual strength. Therefore, I assert that all human beings have the same responsibility as cells to make the human body a functioning entity. The apparent difference is that cells work for the human body as a whole unit, while human beings work for the world as an entity.

If my assertion is true, every human being is uniquely created to fulfill a role designed to benefit the world at large. I will go a step further and state that I firmly believe that every individual is a racial entity unto itself. Today's humans combine several past cultures, some of which we broadly consider ethnic groups. In addition, norms passed down from prior eras through thousands of years of assimilation add to each citizen's uniqueness.

To fully understand the importance of these cultures, there is a need to respect and learn from them. For example, it would be accurate to classify me as a white, septuagenarian Southerner. However, my skin color doesn't fully explain my European origin so a better description would be Caucasian. The fact that I am 76 years of age limits who I am by sometimes dismissing what I learned in my previous 75 years of life.

Classifying me as a Southerner and resident of Cobb County, Georgia, ignores the fact that I lived almost half of my life in New York and Virginia (a state that split in two during the Civil War, with West Virginia becoming a Union state in 1863). In addition, I have English, Dutch, Irish, and some degree of Mediterranean ancestry.

The truth is that I have no complete idea of where I came from if you trace my ancestry back around 6,000 years when civilization, as we know it today, began. Therefore, I would not be true to myself and fair to others if I limited my acceptance and understanding of others to how I see them today. In reality, we are all more than that. We are unique entities with the ability to learn, grow, and be productive citizens who make the world a continually better place.

I have thus far mentioned citizenship in the worldwide context. This book will focus on American citizenship. I maintain that citizenship operating at its highest level in America will transcend to a higher level of citizenship abroad.

I strongly assert that every citizen is unique and responsible for learning and growing to benefit themselves and others. To do this, I would like to introduce my list of areas of responsibility that all citizens must have to be true to themselves and others. I have done this using an acronym: **"REACTION."** This is an appropriate acronym since the definition of reaction is *"an action performed or a feeling experienced in response to a situation or event."* Stated another way, reaction is *"a person's ability to respond physically and mentally to external stimuli."* Citizens react. Effective citizens react in concert with a strong family value system, commitment to learning, adherence to the laws of the land, and respect for and responsibility to others. The eight acronymic headings are as follows:

Respect and Responsibility

Education (Lifetime Learning)

Acceptance

Community (Rules, Laws, and Voting)

Truth & Trust ((Honesty, Integrity, Values)

Industriousness (Diligence)

Operating Value (All human beings are created equal)

Nourishment (Feeding and developing yourself and others)

Respect and Responsibility

Genuine respect for others is vital. This type of respect allows citizens to co-exist effectively. In addition, it builds esteem for the parties involved. Genuine respect contains two characteristics essential to healthy human relations: **LOVE** and **THE GOLDEN RULE.**

Citizens with respect for others convey a significant level of admiration and sense of value toward them. In many cultures, people are worthy of respect until proven otherwise. This practice seems synonymous with a central tenet of American Law: One is innocent until proven guilty.

Citizens must first have self-respect before they can demonstrate genuine respect for others. Respecting yourself means giving and defining your worth and value as a human being. A citizen needs to commit to a practice of self-improvement to develop mind, body, and spirit continually. This practice validates a person's worth as a human being. Unfortunately, not all citizens function at the same level of self-esteem or self-respect. It is crucial to understand this difference, which, in turn, will provide citizens with the patience and willingness to hear opposing views.

Once citizens develop and strengthen their self-respect, they acquire a remarkable ability to respect others. Some of the tools necessary to facilitate this new level of respect are the following:

1. Practice effective listening.

2. Empathize with different opinions.

3. Disagree respectfully.

4. Apologize when you are wrong.

5. Be honest.

6. Fulfill your obligations.

7. Call out disrespectful behavior.

8. Compliment others for their achievements.

Proper respect for others creates the ability to co-exist at a high level. Conversely, a lack of respect carries with it serious consequences. It places citizens at odds with each other. A lack of respect toward others creates barriers instead of bridges.

"Respect for ourselves guides our morals;
respect for others guides our manners."

Lawrence Stone

As citizens understand and practice the art of respect, they are ready to go a step further. The next essential step is an ongoing commitment to treat respect as a fundamental responsibility of your value statement. A lifetime commitment to learning is vital for citizens to grow effectively in changing times.

Education (Lifetime Learning)

Understanding the United States Constitution is an excellent starting point for all citizens to embrace. According to Larry P. Arnn,

President of Hillsdale College: "***The moral foundation of the Constitution is in the Declaration of Independence and its principle of equal rights. Under the Constitution, the government was to be limited to protecting these rights.***" To better understand the meaning of the Constitution, it is vital to study The Federalist Papers. The Federalist Papers are a combination of 85 essays promoting the ratification of the Constitution. Alexander Hamilton wrote 51 papers, followed by James Madison (29) and John Jay (5).

The words of Hamilton, Madison, and Jay cited five critical areas of concern: federalism, checks and balances, separated powers, pluralism, and representation. Although the papers deal with different parts of the government, as noted above, these themes are consistent throughout the collection. For example, the importance of learning the Constitution cited by Lyndon B. Johnson is as follows:

"Our citizens – naturalized or native-born – must also seek to refresh and improve their knowledge of how our government operates under the Constitution and how they can participate in it. Only in this way can they assume the full responsibilities of citizenship and make our government more truly of, by, and for the people."

Effective learning, of course, transcends the acceptance, understanding, and participation in the Constitution. It starts at birth and continues until death. I like to label lifetime learning as something that spans one's "harvest to heaven." A commitment to lifetime learning is the practice of constantly improving oneself. Let us now look at the learning responsibilities of a citizen at various stages of life.

Erick Erickson, a Danish, German-American psychologist, maintained that personality develops in a predetermined order through eight stages of psychological development. I assert that maximizing the learning requirements in each step is critical to developing a complete citizen. Now, let us look at each of these stages.

(1) Infancy (birth to 18 months) – Trust is a significant factor at this stage. A strong level of trust is established if the parent or caregiver meets the child's needs at this stage.

(2) Toddlerhood (18 months to 3 years) – The fundamental issues of developing independence and self-confidence are in this stage.

(3) Pre-school Years (3 years to 5 years) – As children learn independently, they define their purpose in life. Interactions with children roughly the same age facilitate a large portion of the development here.

(4) Early School Years (5 years to 12 years) – This is the stage where children become self-aware and develop critical cognitive skills. If children lack re-enforcement for their accomplishments, they may develop a feeling of inferiority.

(5) Adolescence (12 years to 18 years) – This is a confusing period of self-discovery. Teenagers seek acceptance from their peers during this phase. Therefore, they need to develop healthy relationships in adolescence while accepting the differences in others.

(6) Young Adulthood (18 years to 40 years) – Young adults need to continue to develop healthy relationships throughout this stage. If they don't, they create the possibility of feeling isolated and alone. This sense of isolation impacts their ability to understand the world around them and develop a more substantial virtue of love.

(7) Middle Adulthood (40 years to 65 years) – This is the period where people may choose to rely on what they learned in prior generations, resulting in feelings of unhappiness and resentfulness. If they can instead continue to build on previous learning and become positive and productive community members, they will develop the virtue of care.

(8) Late Adulthood (over 65 years) – This is a time of reflection. If those in this stage are happy with their life, they feel a sense of peace. However, if regrets and failures haunt them, they will likely

experience despair and resentment. The virtue of this stage is wisdom.

Erickson's stages of psychological development define the values associated with each step. These values, in chronological order, are Hope, Will, Purpose, Competence, Fidelity, Capacity to Love, Care, and Wisdom. Each of these values builds upon the ones before it. Therefore, the resultant worth at each stage is fundamental to preparing people for the next step.

All stages of development require formal and informal learning activities. Formal learning is that which is delivered systematically. Informal learning is unstructured and occurs outside of a prescribed educational setting. Formal learning is curriculum-based and occurs in institutions such as schools and colleges. Informal learning occurs through living experiences. I know we have heard of "street smarts vs. book smarts." Effective learning requires a commitment to adhere to a life of learning diligently and respectfully from all sources. This practice will bind citizens to a set of values that can maximize each one's worth.

One organization committed to lifetime learning is Georgia LEARNS LLC, founded ten years ago by Paul Terlemezian, President of iFive Alliances, LLC. The acronym LEARNS stands for Leveraging Every Available Resource Non-stop. Georgia LEARNS LLC focuses on accelerating the ability of other organizations to solve business and social problems in a self-sufficient manner.

I am a charter member of this fine organization that is global and technology-based. During my decade as a member and consultant of Georgia LEARNS, LLC, I have seen it grow through community collaboration. It has also effectively partnered with several entities across the learning spectrum, involved in Pre-K, K-12, Academic, Work, Personal, Military, and Law Enforcement. It has likewise benefitted from the support of for-profit and not-for-profit organizations, large firms, small firms, and entrepreneurs. Georgia LEARNS LLC is a true example of lifetime learning.

No real learning can happen without personal commitment. In the words of Friedrich Nietzsche:

"The doer alone learneth."

Acceptance

According to Tchiki Davis, Ph.D., in an August 2, 2021, article in Psychology Today, acceptance means "taking a stance of non-judgmental awareness and actively embracing the experience of thoughts, feelings, and bodily sensations as they occur" (Hayes et al., 2004). I suggest that effective citizens possess the ability to manage their thoughts, emotions, and actions through this process of acceptance.

The most effective means of problem-solving is first to understand and accept the current situation, providing you with the baseline information necessary to determine the tools required to address the problem. As an example, Alcoholics Anonymous' solution to the treatment of alcoholism is a "12 Step Program." The program's foundation is the first step: acceptance that people are powerless over alcohol and their lives have become unmanageable.

As we move along to discuss the other attributes and responsibilities of an effective citizen, I cannot emphasize enough the importance of laying the foundation for the development of improved citizenship by understanding and accepting the status of your citizenship profile— in other words, one's strengths and weaknesses relative to good citizenship.

Community (Rules, Laws, and Voting)

Once people have accepted their current citizenship profile, they effectively enhance their value to the community. The foundation for a citizen's value statement is strict adherence to community rules and laws.

Establishing community rules or norms that are consistent and understandable to all citizens in the community is vital. These rules and standards direct the behavior of all citizens in the community. In addition, they create a community bond whereby all citizens understand, respect, and follow a consistent set of beliefs and interests. These standards should define community values, articulate goals, prioritize needs, and be inclusive of all citizens.

It is essential to understand, however, that not all citizens may agree with the community rules. Therefore, it is necessary to create a platform where all citizens have an opportunity to voice their differences respectfully. The goal here is to reach an acceptable consensus. Reaching consensus most likely requires substantial "give and take" for some. Therefore, it is crucial to achieve an adequate compromise level during these activities.

A system of community rules becomes a prerequisite for laws that regulate behavior in both public and private societies. These laws take community rules to another level. Laws do the following:

- Set standards for acceptable and unacceptable behavior.

- Provide access to justice and keep everyone safe.

- Establish a system to maintain peace.

- Encourage civil and political engagement.

- Protect the most vulnerable in society.

I see three significant concerns that may negatively impact having an adequate set of Laws. One is that a law may not address the root causes of a problem. The second is a law may not be beneficial to all members of society and only benefit certain groups. The third is some laws may be created to increase power and punish critics.

It is, therefore, essential to enact laws that address the root causes of the problem. If not, the fundamental problem will not be corrected, and the law may, in fact, lead to more harmful results. An example could be a law that punishes illegal drug users and ignores illegal drug providers.

Laws (like community rules) are enacted to apply equally and fairly to all citizens. In the words of Theodore Roosevelt, "***Ours is a government of liberty, by, through and under the Law. No man is above it, and no man below it.***"

Laws created to increase power and punish critics create additional problems for a healthy community. These may come in subtle ways. Examples of laws designed to increase power, to mention only a few, are (1) party gerrymandering and (2) changing voting rules to benefit the political party in charge.

Party gerrymandering is setting the boundaries of electoral districts to favor political interests. This process limits individual freedom in the election process. Furthermore, it is my opinion that political gerrymandering should be unconstitutional. A better method would be to create an independent body to align electoral districts with census results every ten years.

Changing voting rules to benefit a political party creates an unfair power play for the majority party. In 2021, 19 states enacted voting restriction legislation. The alleged purpose of these laws was to cleanse the system of potential voter fraud. However, their actual effect made voting more difficult for some Americans. Such state laws favor the majority party and do not treat all citizens equally.

Moreover, these laws may be legal under the state constitutions but should not apply to Federal elections. This practice will destroy the fairness of the Electoral College and place political parties and not citizens in charge of Presidential elections. I strongly believe in the Electoral College; however, all states must operate under the same rules for Federal elections.

All citizens are entitled to an equal opportunity to participate fairly in the voting process. Furthermore, all citizens are responsible for voting to form a more effective union. Therefore, laws should be structured so that all qualified citizens can exercise their right to vote without undue restrictions. In the words of U.S. Supreme Court Justice Sonia Sotomayor, ***"I firmly believe in the rule of law as a foundation of all our basic rights."***

Truth and Trust (Honesty, Integrity, Values)

We previously discussed the critical values to be learned at various stages of our lives. Furthermore, we discussed how these values collectively build to prepare us for each succeeding phase. Life is full of surprises. Some of these surprises act to support and improve our happiness. However, some surprises impact our lives in negative ways. People who establish and are true to healthy core values develop the tools necessary to cope with all circumstances, positive or negative.

To build on the psychological values cited by Erickson, productive citizens regularly perform value inventories. Moreover, such lists are adjusted throughout life, preparing citizens for the challenges of the times.

All successful organizations prepare two critical statements that guide their activities. One is a Mission Statement, and the other is a Value Statement. The mission statement defines the organization's destination, while the value statement defines its commitment to its stakeholders. Powerful words such as Integrity, Trust, Honesty, Accountability, Diversity, and Humility are part of the value statement of successful organizations. For example, the value proposition of Southwest Airlines goes as far as adding the Golden Rule to its list.

Citizens are not unlike corporations. A fundamental characteristic of a corporation is its existence as a "going concern." Going concern is an accounting term for a company with the resources needed to continue operating indefinitely. Similarly, citizens have the resources necessary to sustain a long life. But, as we know, companies and citizens do not have infinite lives. However, if the success of companies and citizens adds value to their community, this value will transcend their lives and be beneficial well into the future. They will become a vital part of history.

Before we leave this section, I need to briefly discuss the importance of Truth and Trust in all relationships. For citizens to mature, they need to be truthful to themselves. This honesty allows them to build on their successes and learn from their mistakes. A society of citizens also needs to follow this principle. Truthfulness establishes social bonds. Lying and hypocrisy break them.

Trust is also vital to healthy relationships. The dictionary defines trust as a firm belief in the reliability, truth, ability, or strength of someone or something. When we have learned to distrust someone, it is usually because we've come to understand that what we share with them or what's important to us is not safe with that person. A family or community absent of trust is destined for dysfunction. For example, when two parents constantly fight, lie, and secretly do things contrary to the wishes of the other, the trust between them fails. If their children or other relatives and friends witness this, a broader level of trust is likewise doomed to fail.

Steven Covey says it best. "Trust is the glue of life. It's the most essential ingredient in effective communication. It's the fundamental principle that holds all relationships."

Industriousness (Diligence)

Industriousness or perseverance is another fundamental attribute of productive citizens. Hard work and completing tasks are examples of perseverance. A consistent application of this perseverance in all aspects of citizens' endeavors creates and maintains an ethic vital to them. This ethic matures as citizens add a solid commitment to diligence, focusing on the energy necessary to complete a task. An example of diligence is a baseball pitcher studying the tendencies of the batters he will be facing. The pitcher then validates his findings by conferring with the catcher and pitching coach and then modifying his pitching technique accordingly.

Diligent citizens who respect themselves and others are persistent in maintaining a value system that prepares them to co-exist with citizens who may have a different set of values or no values at all. Here, it is crucial to understand the differences between other citizens and yourself. This understanding lays the foundation for compromise or acceptance, despite these differences. Furthermore, this process requires a commitment to listen, educate, and change where required.

"The quality of our lives depends not on whether or not we have conflicts, but on how we respond to them."

Thomas Crum

Thomas Jefferson says, **"Every difference of opinion is not a difference of principle**." He compares "**difference of opinion**" and "**difference of principle**," reminding his audience that they may differ in their opinion, but that does not mean that their principles are different.

These hypotheses of Crum and Jefferson point to vital means to our self-preservation—as individuals, communities, nations, and the global family.

Operating Value: "ALL HUMAN BEINGS ARE CRE-ATED EQUAL."

Thomas Jefferson used "**all men are created equal**" in the Declaration of Independence. This phrase has haunted some American citizens from its inception. America was founded by the diligence and leadership of white men. However, I firmly believe that Jefferson's intent was "humanity" instead of men by gender. In the 200-plus years following the creation of The Declaration of Independence, there have been significant struggles to include rights for women, blacks, Native Americans, differences in sexual orientation, differing religions, and immigrants. The Constitution, Bill of Rights, subsequent Constitutional amendments, and the Civil Rights Act of 1964 all sought to change this oversight. Unfortunately, these struggles still persist today.

I will address the importance of inclusiveness throughout subsequent chapters in this book. Every citizen may be unique, just as the human body cells I referred to earlier. However, this uniqueness can create a common good. Furthermore, synergy occurs once more citizens utilize the attributes or values described in this chapter.

All citizens of this great country are responsible for contributing to powers more significant than themselves. The ultimate authority is God. The citizen's responsibility to God comes from a commitment to spirituality. As citizens exercise their God-given free will and develop a moral and spiritual code, they form the tools necessary to solve more significant problems.

ALL PEOPLE, regardless of gender, skin color, ethnicity, sexual orientation, religion, or where they are from or reside, have equal rights in this great country of ours. Unfortunately, however, some citizens have experienced roadblocks in exercising these rights. These roadblocks impede progress. To make matters worse, somebody intentionally created many of these roadblocks to gain power or money.

We are not here alone. Accordingly, I will repeatedly assert that I believe a citizen's two most important values are **LOVE** of all and

THE GOLDEN RULE. Diligently following these two values will better connect the citizen to the true meaning of **"all human beings are created equal."**

Nourishment (Feeding and Developing Yourself and Others)

Nourishment represents the last letter in the acronym REACTION. It is appropriate since a REACTION to problem-solving is growth and building. Therefore, every citizen constantly feeds the values cited in this chapter to effectively grow and acquire the skills necessary to become a productive member of society.

"This city is what it is because our citizens are what they are."
Plato

As we effectively act and react as productive citizens, it becomes important to bring our focus to charity, which has the effect of lifting others by affording them the tools necessary to become stronger citizens. Positive REACTIONs are enhanced by the gift of charity. Let's now look at charity.

Charity (Helping those in need)

What is charity? I assert it is an example of brotherly love. All citizens have a responsibility to support those who are in need. Charity can take many forms. Kindness is a simple example. Examples are smiling at others, being polite, listening to others, not judging, exercising patience, and extending compassion. Another is to give of one's time, talent, and treasure. Donating one's available assets either directly or through an organization is an example of this type of charity.

Other means of charity require diligence. The following are examples of this:

- Compliment others when appropriate.

- Stop for those in need.

- Help someone across the road or with groceries.

- Give someone directions.

- Offer to pay for someone's food or drink.

- Help an elderly neighbor.

- Teach others.

- Help someone with a disabled car.

The act of charity adds value to our lives. It also provides a method of strengthening social connections. I have a personal experience that describes this.

In 1991, I was one week into a new job at a non-profit organization. As I began to drive home, someone who appeared distressed approached me as I was waiting for a streetlight to change. This person flagged me down and stated that he was driving a vanload of kids to an event and ran out of gas. Unfortunately, since he came down a hill, I couldn't see the van he described. He asked if he could "borrow" a few dollars to buy enough gas to fulfill his mission. I hesitated and assessed the situation as follows: (1) he is conning me, and I will be a sucker for giving him money; or (2) he is telling the truth, requiring someone to help him. I decided on the latter and gave him $10. He wanted my address to repay the money; however, I told him it was a gift and wished the kids and him all the best.

I was a Certified Financial Planner before accepting my current job. One of my clients was a Vietnamese doctor I had met a year earlier. I received a call from the Vietnamese doctor a month after making the gift referred to above. He stated that he wanted to pay me for my past service to him. I responded that he didn't owe me anything. He said he recognized that; however, he wanted me to have a gift as a reward for the courtesy and respect I demonstrated during our relationship. Even though I assured him this wasn't necessary, he sent me $1,000.

I do not know what the van driver (or con man) did with my $10. But I believe the universe rewarded the Vietnamese doctor and me for it. I worked 20 more years in the non-profit field with joy and satisfaction. After retirement, I started volunteering at a senior living facility, which has added even more value to my life.

The following quote by Mother Teresa best describes my understanding of charity.

"Let no one ever come to you without leaving better and happier. Be the living expression of God's kindness: kindness in your face, kindness in your eyes, kindness in your smile."

Chapter Three

Quotes on Citizenship

As we move forward in our journey to show the effect of good citizenship on our individual growth and the growth of those around us (family, community, nation, and foreign nations), it is important to see how prominent citizens have reflected on the importance of good citizenship. I have done this through famous quotes from three groups: (1) US Presidents, (2) Founding Fathers, and (3) Other Distinguished People.

I believe that you will find significant elements of REACTION in these quotes.

As you will see, I have provided one quote from each President. Many citizens, both past and present, have strong feelings about the effectiveness of their respective tenures in office. This mostly comes from the citizens' political party leanings, their dependence on information taken from outside sources, their upbringing, the quality of their education, etc.

If we accept these Presidential quotes as coming not from a political leader but from the Chief Executive of our nation who is striving to fulfill his oath of office, we will get a clearer picture of their understanding of the importance of good citizenship.

Presidential Quotes

"It is now no more that toleration is spoken of, as if it was by the indulgence of one class of people, that another enjoyed the exercise of their inherent natural rights, for, happily, the government of the United States, which gives to bigotry no sanction, to persecution no assistance, requires only that they who live under its protection should demean themselves as good citizens."

George Washington

"You will ever remember that all the End of study is to make you a good man and a useful Citizen."

John Adams

"A nation, as a society, forms a moral person, and every member of it is personally responsible for his society."

Thomas Jefferson

"That the foundation of our national policy should be laid in private morality. If individuals be not influenced by moral principles, it is in vain to look for public virtue; it is, therefore, the duty of legislators to enforce, both by precept and example, the utility, as well as the necessity, of a strict adherence to the rules of distributive justice."

James Madison

"In a representative republic, the education of our children must be of the utmost importance!"

James Monroe

"Try and fail, but don't fail to try."

John Quincy Adams

"Every good citizen makes his country's honor his own, and cherishes it not only as precious but as sacred. He is willing to risk his life in its defense and is conscious that he gains protection while he gives it."

Andrew Jackson

"There is a power in public opinion in this country – and I thank God for it: for it is the most honest and best of all powers – which will not tolerate an incompetent or unworthy man to hold in his weak or wicked hands the lives and fortunes of his fellow-citizens."

Martin Van Buren

"Sound morals, religious liberty, and a just sense of religious responsibility are essentially connected with all true and lasting happiness."

William Henry Harrison

"The institutions under which we live, my countrymen, secure each person in the perfect enjoyment of all his rights."

John Tyler

"All distinctions of birth or of rank have been abolished. All citizens, whether native or adopted, are placed upon terms of precise equality. All are entitled to equal rights and equal protection."

James K. Polk

"The only ground of hope for the continuance of our free institutions is in the proper moral and religious training of the children, that they may be prepared to discharge aright the duties of men and citizens."

Zachary Taylor

"Nations, like individuals in a state of nature, are equal and independent, possessing certain rights and owing certain duties to each other."

Millard Fillmore

"While men inhabiting different parts of this vast continent cannot be expected to hold the same opinions, they can unite in a common objective and sustain common principles."

Franklin Pierce

"The ballot box is the surest arbiter of disputes among free men."

James Buchanan

"Let us at all times remember that all American citizens are brothers of a common country, and should dwell together in bonds of fraternal feeling."

Abraham Lincoln

"The life of a republic lies certainly in the energy, virtue, and intelligence of its citizens."

Andrew Johnson

"If we are to have another contest in the near future of our national existence, I predict that the dividing line will not be Mason and Dixon's but between patriotism and intelligence on the one side, and superstition, ambition and ignorance on the other."

Ulysses S. Grant

"Crimes increase as education, opportunity, and property decrease. Whatever spreads ignorance, poverty and, discontent causes crime.... Criminals have their own responsibility, their own share of guilt, but they are merely the hand.... Whoever interferes with equal rights and equal opportunities is in some real degree, responsible for the crimes committed in the community."

Rutherford B. Hayes

"Now more than ever the people are responsible for the character of their Congress. If that body be ignorant, reckless, and corrupt, it is because the people tolerate ignorance, recklessness, and corruption. If it be intelligent, brave, and pure, it is because the people demand these high qualities to represent them in the national legislature. . . . If the next centennial does not find us a great nation . . . it will be because those who represent the enterprise, the culture, and the morality of the nation do not aid in controlling the political forces."

James A. Garfield

"Be fit for more than the thing you are now doing. Let everyone know that you have a reserve in yourself; that you have more power than you are now using. If you are not too large for the place you occupy, you are too small for it."

Chester A. Arthur

"A government for the people must depend for its success on the intelligence, the morality, the justice, and the interest of the people themselves."

Grover Cleveland

"That one flag encircles us with its folds today, the unrivaled object of our loyal love."

Benjamin Harrison

"The mission of the United States is one of benevolent assimilation."

William McKinley

"Begin with the little thing, and do not expect to accomplish anything without an effort."

Theodore Roosevelt

"The man with the average mentality, but with control, with a definite goal, and a clear conception of how it can be gained, and above all, with the power of application and labor, wins in the end."

William Howard Taft

"We are citizens of the world. The tragedy of our times is that we do not know this."

Woodrow Wilson

"We need citizens who are less concerned about what their government can do for them, and more concerned about what they can do for the nation."

Warren G. Harding

"It is not in violence and crime that our greatest danger lies. These evils are so perfectly apparent that they very quickly arouse the moral power of the people for their suppression. A far more serious danger lurks in the shirking of those responsibilities of citizenship, where the evil may not be so noticeable but is more insidious and likely to be more devastating."

Calvin Coolidge

"It is a paradox that every dictator has climbed to power on the ladder of free speech. Immediately on attaining power, each dictator has suppressed all free speech except his own."

Herbert Hoover

"We must scrupulously guard the civil rights and civil liberties of all our citizens, whatever their background. We must remember that any oppression, any injustice, any hatred, is a wedge designed to attack our civilization."

Franklin D. Roosevelt

"Work Hard. Do your best. Keep your word. Never get too big for your britches. Trust in God. Have no fear; and Never forget a friend."

Harry S. Truman

"We the people, elect leaders not to rule but to serve."

Dwight D. Eisenhower

"My fellow Americans, ask not what your country can do for you, ask what you can do for your country."

John F. Kennedy

"The guns and the bombs, the rockets and the warships, are all symbols of human failure."

Lyndon B. Johnson

"We cannot learn from one another until we stop shouting at one another – until we speak quietly enough so that our words can be heard as well as our voices."

Richard M. Nixon

"America now is stumbling through the darkness of hatred and divisiveness. Our values, our principles, and our determination to succeed as a free and democratic people will give us a torch to light the way. And we will survive and become the stronger – not only because of a patriotism that stands for love of country, but a patriotism that stands for love of people."

Gerald R. Ford

"We have become not a melting pot but a beautiful mosaic. Different people, different beliefs, different yearnings, different hopes, different dreams."

Jimmy Carter

"Good citizenship and defending democracy means living up to the ideals and values that make this country great."

Ronald Reagan

"I have spoken of a thousand points of light, of all the community organizations that are spread like stars throughout the Nation, doing good."

George H. W. Bush

"There is nothing wrong with America that cannot be cured by what is right with America."

Bill Clinton

"As young Americans, you have an important responsibility, which is to become good citizens."

George W. Bush

"In the face of impossible odds, people who love this country can change it."

Barack Obama

"When America is united, America is unstoppable."

Donald Trump

"Our future cannot depend on government alone. The ultimate solutions lie in the attitudes and the actions of the American people."

Joe Biden

Quotes From Founding Fathers

The following are quotes related to citizenship from certain Founding Fathers, excluding those from four Presidents who were also Founding Fathers and quoted in the section above.

"Liberty will not long survive the total extinction of morals."

Samuel Adams

"If everyone is thinking alike, then no one is thinking."

Benjamin Franklin

"The people alone have an incontestable, unalienable, and indefeasible right to institute government and to reform, alter, or totally change the same when their protection, safety, prosperity, and happiness require it."

Alexander Hamilton

"Though we are politically enemies, yet with regard to Science it is presumable we shall not dissent from the practice of civilized people in promoting it."

John Hancock

"United we stand, divided we fall. Let us not split into factions which must destroy that union upon which our existence hangs."

Patrick Henry

"To all general purposes, we have uniformly been one people; each individual citizen everywhere enjoying the same national rights, privileges, and protection."

John Jay

"That no free government, nor the blessings of liberty, can be preserved to any people, but by a firm adherence to justice, moderation, temperance, frugality, and virtue; by frequent recurrence to fundamental principles; and by the recognition by all citizens that they have duties as well as rights, and that such rights cannot be enjoyed save in a society where law is respected and due process is observed."

George Mason

"I am not one of those politicians that run testy when my own plans are not adopted. I think it is the duty of a good citizen to follow when he cannot lead."

Robert Morris

"I will never be a tool in the hands of the King to work my own dishonor or that of my country."

Peyton Randolph

"The question is not what rights naturally belong to man, but how they may be most equally and effectually guarded in society."

Roger Sherman

Citizenship Quotes from Other Distinguished People

"It is not always the same thing to be a good man and a good citizen."

Aristotle

"Never doubt that a small group of thoughtful, committed citizens can change the world; indeed, it's the only thing that ever has."

Margaret Mead

"The only title in our democracy superior to that of President is the title of citizen."

Louis D. Brandeis

"Be the compromise you want to see in the world."

Mahatma Gandhi

"Our citizenship in the United States is our national character. Our citizenship in any particular state is only our local distinction. By the latter we are known at home, by the former to the world. Our great title is AMERICANS."

Thomas Paine

"The right of every American to first-class citizenship is the most important issue of our time."

Jackie Robinson

"Whatever makes men good Christians, makes them good citizens."

Daniel Webster

"As citizens of this democracy, you are the rulers and the ruled, the law-givers and the law-abiding, the beginning and the end."

Adlai E. Stevenson

"No country can really develop unless its citizens are educated."

Nelson Mandela

"This city is what it is because our citizens are what they are."

Plato

"No one is born a good citizen; no nation is born a democracy. Rather, both are processes that continue to evolve over a lifetime. Young people must be included from birth. A society that cuts off from its youth severs its lifeline."

Kofi Annan

"Active citizenship begins with an envisioning of the desired outcome and a conscious application of spiritual principles."

Dennis Kucinich

"Citizenship is what makes a republic; monarchies can get along without it."

Mark Twain

For this book, my goal is for you, the readers, to try to remove yourselves from the obstacles that may prevent you from an objective response to the principles within. A few of these are political bias, religious and racial differences, generational gaps, educational disparity, etc. I am confident that you will be able to find a way to merge such differences into a better concept of citizenship without sacrificing your beliefs and other differences.

In the next chapter, I will describe the building blocks necessary to become an effective citizen.

Chapter Four

My Growth as a Citizen

As I have stated earlier, I see myself as just an ordinary person. However, I consider myself an important player in the universe of human existence. Earlier, I referred to a cell in the human body as analogous to a person as a vital part of the world around it. That being my premise, I believe any ordinary person can function effectively with others to attain a higher-level of mutual existence.

We have always lived in challenging times. America has fought its way to independence as a country. America abolished slavery and spent the better part of the next two decades attempting to cure the poison that slavery had infused into our hearts and souls. America has endured a civil war where it sacrificed over 600,000 impassioned citizens and divided us in a way that almost ended the single political entity of the United States. Subsequently, America was a vital participant in two World Wars, the Spanish-American War and the Mexican-American War, and conflicts in Korea, Vietnam, Iraq, and Afghanistan. America has dealt with differences that had the potential to lead to a nuclear holocaust. And today… America is fighting to maintain its role as a major economic power and leader in the free world.

As in past generations, citizens today may see their challenges as too big to overcome (depression), too complex to understand (ignorance), something to ignore (lack of responsibility), or a challenge that must be addressed in a manner conducive to a person's capabilities (good citizenship).

In this book, I will not be looking for solutions to America's problems or those of the rest of the world. Instead, my focus will center on the capacity of an individual to make a positive contribution through good citizenship, resulting in positive changes to the world at large. These simple tools will strive to enable the individual to impart a positive impact on their family, enrich their value to the community, and, by replication, improve America and the world around it.

In the late 1970s, Lyall Watson documented the research findings of several Japanese primatologists on the Island of Koshima in the 1950s. His work was referred to as the "hundredth monkey effect," as it demonstrated the importance of learning activities in one group setting that are capable of being copied in other group settings. I am convinced that Watson's work here can lead to an exponential increase in effective citizenship. His report on the findings is as follows:

The original Koshima research was undertaken by a team of scientists as a secondary consequence of 1948 research on semi-wild monkeys in Japan. The Koshima troop was identified and segregated from other monkeys and, from 1950, used as a closed study group to observe wild Japanese macaque behavior. While studying the group, the team would drop sweet potatoes and wheat on the beach and observe the troop's behavior. In 1954, a paper was published indicating the first observances of one monkey, Imo, washing her sweet potatoes in the water.

Her changed behavior led to several feeding behavior changes over the course of the next few years, all of which were of great benefit in understanding the process of teaching and learning in animal behavior. A brief account of the behavioral changes can be seen below:

- The young first teach their contemporaries and immediate family, who all benefit from the new behavior and teach it to their contemporaries.
- If the parents or their contemporaries (or their parents) are too old, they do not adopt the behavior.

- Once the initial group has children, a change occurs in the dynamic of the behavior from teaching previous and current generations to a new dynamic where the next generation learns by observation. The behavior is no longer actively taught but passively observed and mimicked.

- The first innovator continues to innovate. The young monkey who started potato washing also learned how to sift wheat grains out of the sand by throwing handfuls of sand and wheat into the water and then catching the wheat that floated to the top. This behavior was also copied using the above teaching and learning process until there were too many monkeys on the island with too little wheat apportioned, which is when competition became too fierce, and the stronger monkeys would steal the collected wheat from the weaker ones, so they stopped the learned behavior in self-preservation.

- The innovator's sibling started another innovation, whereas the monkeys were initially fearful of the ocean, only deciding to put their hands and feet into it. The wheat-straining innovation led to monkeys submerging more of their bodies in the water or play-splashing in the ocean. This behavior was again copied using the above teaching and learning processes.

The study does not indicate a catalyst ratio at which all the Koshima monkeys started washing sweet potatoes or a correlation to other monkey studies where similar behavior started. On the contrary, it indicated that certain age groups in Koshima would not learn the behavior.

Ken Keyes Jr. further popularized this story with the publication of his book *The Hundredth Monkey* (1984). Keyes' book was about the devastating effects of nuclear war on the planet. Keyes presented the "hundredth monkey effect" story as an inspirational parable, applying it to human society and the impact of positive change.

Keyes' work was challenged partially because it incorporated too many of his political beliefs into his work and thereby offended many. However, I am convinced that there is no doubt that the "hundredth monkey effect" has the capacity to inspire a nation of citizens to effect positive change.

Unlike Keyes, I will not use this book to argue my political beliefs. However, I will strive to show how one person can positively change the environment by consistently doing the right thing.

Over time, all people develop beliefs that guide their functioning connection to those who engage them. These beliefs are learned from family, institutions of formal education, personal acquaintances, religious institutions, work relationships, experiences with friends, reactions to those who disagree with them, etc. As these are learned beliefs, they have a capacity to be modified in response to new circumstances. The world is constantly changing through technological developments, advancements in the ability to improve self-learning, and, as a result, one ever more populous generation after another.

Personally, I have a strong belief that two principles can act as catalysts to improve ourselves and those around us. They are LOVE and THE GOLDEN RULE. These are thoughts and actions that are the foundation of a value system that is capable of positively influencing one's existence and that of others.

Why are these principles so important? The act of LOVE leads to a sense of belonging. THE GOLDEN RULE leads to good morals. The Gospel of Matthew cited this as a Christian's duty with the precept, ***"In everything, do to others what you would have them do to you."***

Without LOVE, a positive sense of belonging cannot exist. As a result, without a sense of belonging, there is a negative impact on one's mental and physical health and one's happiness and longevity. Variations of THE GOLDEN RULE span several civilizations, possibly dating back to ancient Egypt in 2000 BC. Christians embraced it as a proclamation in Jesus' Sermon on the Mount. All forms are seen as a key principle of morality and an ethical duty to those around us.

As citizens age, become more educated, and acquire additional life experiences, their value to themselves and others will be strongly enhanced by the ability to LOVE themselves and others and to apply THE GOLDEN RULE to their decision-making. I constantly remind my grandsons of the importance of these principles and hope they grow up with them as part of their value systems. The following are some quotes on LOVE:

"Love conquers all."

Virgil, in the 1st century BC

"The giving of love is an education in itself."

Eleanor Roosevelt

"The first duty of love is to listen."

Paul Tillich

"The best proof of love is trust."

Dr. Joyce Brothers

"Love is the only force capable of transforming an enemy into a friend."

Martin Luther King, Jr.

Some Quotes on *THE GOLDEN RULE*

"Never do to others what you would not like them to do to you."

Confucius

"Do not do to others what angers you if done to you by others."

Socrates

"Practicing the golden rule is not a sacrifice, it is an investment."

Byllye Avery

"The golden rule of conduct is mutual toleration, seeing that we will never all think alike, and we shall see Truth in fragments and from different angles of vision."

Mahatma Gandhi

"If you contemplate The Golden Rule, it turns out to be an injunction to live by grace rather than what you think other people deserve."

Deepak Chopra

With LOVE and THE GOLDEN RULE as the foundation of a robust value system, we can now take a journey through the growth of a good citizen.

Let us start with education as the foundation for good citizenship.

Education is comprised of two important disciplines: teaching and learning. In formal education structures, one teacher is responsible for the learning of many. This structure continues from pre-K through high school, college, and beyond. A variation of this is present in the business world as well as the military.

It is important to note that informal education opportunities are constantly occurring. This occurs at the family dinner table, when one socializes with friends and new acquaintances, reads or watches news on television, surfs the worldwide web, etc. The effectiveness of this type of education depends on how the latest information is presented and its truthfulness. Therefore, it is vitally important for the learner to not only understand what is presented to them but to be diligent enough to evaluate its truthfulness.

As informal learning opportunities present themselves, quite often, the structure is the opposite of formal structures. There may be many teachers and one learner. Therefore, I believe the effectiveness of a person's learning is their own responsibility. It is important here for the learner to be constantly on guard for cult thinking, group thinking, and majority wickedness. As groups form a bond and endeavor to invite others into their views and goals, the learner must beware of the group's (teacher's) motives. Are they based on truth, honesty, love, and a commitment to improve the lives of all persons in the extended group? If not, consider tempering your initial interest and study the group further.

A fundamental premise of mine is that learning is dysfunctional if it comes from a teacher or teachers who have poor values and are received by a learner without a positive value system. Eventually, the learner routinely disseminates what they have learned to others. On the contrary, good citizen learners will vet their new information and determine if it is worth presenting to others and, if so, do it with honesty and a spirit of love designed to make you and the receiver of the information better citizens.

Learning starts in infancy, with the teaching and nurturing coming almost exclusively from parents, with the assistance of grandparents and other family members. The child has no choice other than to trust his teachers. The value system of the teacher (i.e., parents and immediate family), therefore, is a significant influence on an infant as it advances to a toddler. Therefore, parents who administer nurturing techniques of love, respect, honesty, and fairness have made the first and most important step toward developing their children into good citizens.

As the child grows and experiences other situations, the effectiveness of their self-learning becomes vitally important. These situations present learning opportunities that may require the child to respond to occurrences that they are not equipped to handle. Therefore, their learned and applied value system will provide them with a roadmap toward positive decision-making. If this value system has a foundation of LOVE and THE GOLDEN RULE, the child will have essential tools to address different circumstances.

Let me take my life as an example.

I was born in a small town in Virginia in 1947. As an infant, my father abandoned me. As a matter of fact, his family tried to convince my mother to abort me. My nurturing grandmother would have no part of it and told my mother that she would love the opportunity to introduce me to life in my new world. My mother decided to accept my grandmother's offer.

On a side note, the feeling of family love that resulted from their decision to give me life eventually provided me with a view on abortion. Without tackling the topic of abortion in totality (not the goal of this book), my view relates to the following: If there is a likelihood that the child can be successfully raised without danger to the mother, there is little or no (non-medical) reason to abort. In my case, my father was too irresponsible, as well as part of a family who was too selfish to participate in my growth. As a result, I can't see selfishness or a lack of responsibility as a good reason for an abortion.

The topic of abortion is too complex for me to discuss in this book. I only wanted to present my feelings regarding the decision-making in my case.

As I was growing up, I lived with my grandmother because my mother moved to New York City so that she could earn more money from her career as a registered nurse. Therefore, I would only see my mother two to three times a year (usually a week in the summer, possibly my birthday and Christmas). Unlike my father's direct abandonment, I eventually felt a feeling of indirect abandonment from my mother. I never questioned her love for me, however.

The household that I grew up in consisted of my grandfather, grandmother, and Uncle Jack (my mother's brother). My grandmother was the instrumental female figure in my growth, and Uncle Jack was the closest example of a father figure through high school. They both were pure-hearted, full of love, and anxious to introduce me, as best they could, to all the positive things I required to become a good person.

In addition to the love and support I received from my grandmother (Mama Kitty) and Uncle Jack, some harmful activities existed in the household. My grandfather and his youngest son (the fun-loving uncle I enjoyed playing with) were alcoholics. Other negative influences that I won't get into in this book also presented themselves in our household.

As I grew, I developed low self-esteem. I constantly felt others who had a traditional family life (as I saw it) were better than me. I was also the smallest and youngest boy in my class, which allowed others to tease me and keep me at the bottom of their list to play on their sports teams. The dysfunction in my own household added to this. However, thanks to Mama Kitty and Uncle Jack, I developed some positive tools to neutralize these feelings.

The exposure that Mama Kitty and Uncle Jack gave me allowed me to understand the importance of education and the feeling of belonging. Uncle Jack introduced me to sports (bowling, golf, and baseball). Even though I was small, I made my Little League team and was a starter. I played on my high school golf team and bowled in an adult bowling league. I wasn't a great student, but Mama Kitty kept me on task and provided me with an understanding of the importance of education.

In their own way, Mama Kitty, Uncle Jack, and even my mother provided me with love and nurturing so that I could grow with many of the tools necessary to become a good citizen. I was a naughty young lad and sometimes rebelled against their teachings. As I grew older, I saw a value system that was the core of their teachings. These centered around LOVE, the importance of education, respect, truth, honesty, and, of course, THE GOLDEN RULE.

The next critical period of the development of a good citizen is during formal education, where two important activities are present:

(1) parent/teacher relationships and (2) relations with classmates and others.

The relationships between students and parents and students and teachers become vitally important to the positive development of the student into not only an educated but a well-rounded member of the school universe.

The first and probably most important part of these is effective communication, allowing an alliance between parents and teachers. With a strong commitment to good communication, the parents and the teachers can bridge the gap between their individual knowledge about the student. It is, therefore, crucial for the parents and teachers to work as allies by accepting their responsibilities to the student. This can only be effectively done in a value-based environment centered on honesty, respect, and diligence.

It should be noted that, on the side of the parents, the more dismissed they feel by the teacher, the less likely they are to participate in the student's education. Furthermore, on the teacher's side, the less the feeling of being heard, the more likely they will stop communicating with the parents.

To further emphasize the importance of the alliance mentioned above, let's examine the elements of the information gap referred to above.

On the home side, there are all the things that parents know about their child, such as the amount of help they provide with their homework and the student's social development with siblings, other family members, and peers. On the school side, there are all the things the teacher knows about them, such as the help they are getting with their schoolwork and their social development with their peers at school. This is analogous to balancing a checkbook, which can only be done effectively by bridging the gap between the information known by the bank and that known by the bank account holder. During my adult years, I spent decades as an accountant, so I couldn't help using this analogy. Sorry!

The knowledge gained from a respectful and honest parent/teacher relationship can be combined to create a fuller understanding of the student. This is not only a benefit to the student but also to the parents and teachers.

Obviously, all students are unique in some ways. As a result, there will always be some students who develop school-refusal behaviors. Even though they are a small segment of the school population, they must be addressed promptly. An honest parent/teacher relationship can result in a solution that is beneficial to the growth and development of those students.

Relationships between the student and their classmates, as well as other associations, also impact the student's development. Effective social relationships are vital to the child's growth. They may come from interaction with classmates, siblings, parents, other relatives, friends, and acquaintances.

Some of these interactions occur in a structured environment (family, classroom, church, etc.), while some take place in unstructured atmospheres such as school restrooms, with friends on the playground, at the mall, play dates, etc. All these relationships are vital to the growth of a child. Through these, they will experience positive and negative activities that will influence their development and their value system.

During these interactions, the values of LOVE and THE GOLDEN RULE become extremely important. With the application of these values, the child will have the ability to see right vs wrong better and develop a positive way to respond to the situation.

We have heard the term **"It Takes a Village"** to describe all the needs required to raise a child. I strongly embrace this saying. As the child develops, unexpected situations will occur that will impact the growth of the child. It is important here that loving role models are present to round out the child's growth.

With the reader's indulgence, I will now explore some of these situations through my life experiences.

While I was growing up in a small town, I had several folks watching over me. They were Mama Kitty, Uncle Jack, teachers, close friends, other family members, neighbors, etc. Even though, as I mentioned earlier, some of my family members had their own issues to deal with, I cannot question their love for me. Therefore, while my non-traditional family life may have been cluttered with dysfunction, the love for me was always present.

Even though there were so many people who cared about me, I still ran into situations where I was alone and unprepared for the consequences. Keep in mind that during these situations, I was young, ignorant of the elements of the situation, small in stature, cute (if I may say so myself), shy, with low self-esteem, having the desire for inclusion, and a tendency to be mischievous.

The first situation occurred when I was around five years old. On a side note, there was no pre-K or kindergarten in my county at that time (1952). I was playing Tarzan. Therefore, I thought it would be more realistic if I was naked when I climbed my favorite tree. I later discovered while I was up this tree in my birthday suit, that I had made a big mistake. I looked down and saw Mama Kitty with a switch in her hand. She not only explained to me a little about the importance of privacy, but she also put a few marks on me that helped me remember her teaching.

I now see this as a funny learning experience. However, without the diligence of a neighbor who saw me and told my grandmother, I most likely would have continued this activity with potentially harmful results.

My first year in formal education was the 1ˢᵗ grade. Three significant events happened during that year. First, to gain popularity, I robbed Mama Kitty's penny jar, which was like a small savings account for her. In an attempt to gain acceptance from my friends, I used the funds to buy candy for them and me. Subsequently, the local merchant told Mama Kitty, and I think you know the rest.

Secondly, my friends and I noticed a windmill that was on our way to school. One day after school, to have fun and to show our (false) lack of fear, we climbed the windmill. Once we reached the top, we all realized that we were scared, resulting in our inability to go down. After a while, word reached my grandfather, who climbed up and safely helped us all down. As a result of the candy and windmill incidents, I started to question my decision-making. Also, when Mama Kitty found out about this, my mistakes became indelibly clear.

Thirdly, during recess, while my classmates and I were playing, a few decided to play a joke on the little guy. I was captured and held down by some of them while one of them urinated on me. To this day, I don't remember if I cited the ones who did it, but I couldn't escape the smell and wetness of my clothes when I returned to the classroom. As a result, I believe they sent me home for the rest of the day so I could change and adjust to the circumstances. This occurrence bothered me for years. Powerlessness, anger, shame, and lack of trust became a part of me well into my adulthood. The depth of the impact that this experience had on me was something that neither my teachers, Mama Kitty, nor Uncle Jack were qualified to address. They tried, however.

The next event was psychologically traumatic. It happened when I was ten or eleven years of age. I had a cousin who was three to five years older than me, who I was accustomed to playing with at our homes. On one occasion, he decided to introduce me to something I was totally unprepared for. This resulted in inappropriate touching each other and my participation in something I was not ready for nor understood in any way. My cousin kept this up with me for many months (maybe years, I don't recall). I was a pawn in his game of sex. What made it worse was that I was too embarrassed to tell anyone.

My cousin later brought a friend of his into the activities so I could "watch and learn." I didn't know what sex was and especially had no understanding of gay sex. I was a prisoner of their games. Somehow, I later escaped these activities and never participated in anything like them again. However, again, I developed feelings of powerlessness, anger, shame, and a lack of trust, which became a part of me indefinitely.

I felt the loneliness derived from this experience all through the rest of middle school and throughout high school. I noticed that many people around me laughed at queers (as they were identified then). I became too shy to date. In fact, my first date was a drive-in movie with a classmate named Mary, where an older female cousin of mine drove us and acted as chaperone. We were in the 9th grade. We had a good time, and we wanted to date each other again.

Mary was also the niece of Uncle Jack's best friend, who was a regular golf partner of Uncle Jack and me. The next time we were hoping to date was on a trip to the roller rink. The roller rink was approximately 15 miles from our house, and the trip was to be comprised of around five or six teenagers. To my displeasure, Mama Kitty refused to allow me to go. As it turned out, a tragedy occurred when, on the way home, the car carrying my friends, Mary among them, ran into a lumber truck. Several passengers were killed, including Mary.

This incident hit many of us very hard, including Mary's family, our family, other students, and friends, and especially me. I never dated again throughout high school, even though there may have been opportunities. I didn't go to the prom or other dances. As much as I wanted to have a healthy relationship with a female friend, I couldn't.

I never learned to drive until after high school, and even though some girls were good candidates for companionship, I never felt qualified to provide them happiness. I was lost. Again, I felt alone and didn't see myself worthy of a healthy relationship with someone else. This didn't change until I experienced more of life's lessons down the road. It was becoming clear that my future happiness required considerable change in my thinking and feelings.

Now, I was at a point where I hoped that a change in environment would provide me with a clean slate and enable me to capture happiness through new experiences. Even though my family life was non-traditional and many of my early life experiences were traumatic, I had hope that a physical change in the environment would conquer all. I was wrong.

I graduated high school, and I was still the youngest and smallest person in my class. I was also an average student, and as a result, my college choices were limited. In the end, I accepted an opportunity to enter a small college in a neighboring state. Things initially went well. I was getting good grades and even had time to try to qualify for the school bowling team (I made the team as an alternate). The satisfaction I received from this experience provided me with the hope I could make the golf team in the spring.

Then, something happened that contributed to a change in my life that burdened me for two and a half decades.

I STARTED DRINKING ALCOHOLIC BEVERAGES.

I never drank before this, mainly because Uncle Jack didn't drink, and Mama Kitty wouldn't allow booze in her house. I was exposed to it in other settings but never imbibed it. This all changed at college on my 18th birthday. A party that centered around beer and grain alcohol created an atmosphere of (out of control) drinking that I couldn't resist. The result was dramatic. I became uncontrollably drunk, and as the party expanded to the street, my activities resulted in my arrest and a night in jail.

My incarceration was recorded in the local newspaper and was seen by the President of the college. As a result, I was forced to leave the institution. However, they were kind enough not to put it on my record. I then had to tell my mother and my stepdad of two years. Embarrassment and parent scolding followed. This resulted in me living with my parents in New York City.

Since my stepfather drank a lot and my mother enjoyed cocktails, I never received discouragement from drinking. This resulted in a feeling that drinking was OK for me and would enhance my happiness.

I have mentioned these experiences, some cute and some traumatic, to make an important point. Regardless of the good messages delivered to you by your parents, primary caregivers, teachers, and other members of the community, unexpected situations will occur, and, as a result, the child must adapt to the new experiences and learn on their own.

Self-education, in connection with a solid value system, is the ingredient that forms the foundation for a good citizen. No matter how much a child receives good information, the child must interpret this information and, hopefully, react positively to the messages received.

For people to grow solidly through the positive messages they receive, they must accept the responsibility for learning the message and for their actions that result from disobeying the lessons they received.

When this happens, the person takes important steps toward building character and becoming a good citizen. This doesn't happen automatically. There will be trial and error, false starts, and even rebellion.

If I had better understood, during these times, that I had the responsibility to create a positive atmosphere in my decision-making, my citizenship-building would have accelerated at a faster pace.

There were critical character-building lessons available to me in the personal experiences I previously cited. Let us explore some of them.

First, my life was almost terminated because of an abortion. Obviously, I had no control over this. However, my value system was enhanced by the way my mother and Mama Kitty acted under the circumstances. Eventually, I took away character-building gems such as responsibility, the importance of caring for others, and especially LOVE and THE GOLDEN RULE.

Second, my Tarzan experience can be described as a cute playing experience for a young child. However, it was a child's game played without an understanding of its surroundings. By the way, even Tarzan wore a loin cloth. Mama Kitty, initially, and my future experiences added some life lessons that I needed. I knew it was wrong to be naked in public, but I didn't think anyone would notice. (I also didn't have a loin cloth.) Lessons of self-respect, dignity, responsibility to others, and community protocol were taught. There were also strong elements of LOVE and THE GOLDEN RULE.

Third, Mama Kitty's penny jar robbery had a lasting effect on my growth. The naughty side of me took over my decision-making here. I knew it was wrong to steal. I also knew what Mama Kitty would do to me if she found out. This didn't deter me. I wanted to be a hero with my friends and share my newly found wealth with them. As it turned out, the store owner told my grandmother. I don't remember if the candy that I bought made me sick, but I do remember the painful message I received from Mama Kitty.

From this experience, I learned the importance of the Fifth and Eighth of God's Commandments. I also broke specific community and family standards by failing to honor known rules, being dishonest, lacking respect for others, and teaching my friends a bad message. Oh, by the way, I failed to show LOVE and didn't follow THE GOLDEN RULE.

My "Don Quixote" experience with the windmill taught me a lesson on safety and the danger associated with bad decisions. Not only could we have fallen and been seriously injured (or worse), but I also involved my grandfather in the situation and put him in jeopardy. Again, my mischievous ways, lack of self-respect, and unwillingness to follow community rules got me into trouble. If I showed LOVE for myself and others and followed THE GOLDEN RULE by not doing something to put others at risk, I would have learned in greater depth my two vital lessons on good citizenship.

My traumatic experience of being held and urinated on had a psychological impact on me. I don't remember now, but I believe I may have initially provoked one of the culprits by teasing him. This should have been a lesson for me. The greater messages that I received took years to overcome. They were the shame I felt, the feeling of powerlessness that overcame me, the anger I had toward my friends, my loss of self-respect, and, encompassing all of this, a feeling of worthlessness. These scars stayed with me for many years and strongly impacted my growth. Obviously, a lack of LOVE and THE GOLDEN RULE prevailed in this instance.

The sexual abuse by my older cousin haunted me for decades. What he did to me was selfish, with total disregard for its impact on my mind and physical growth. I don't know, but I believe it also had to be illegal. Fortunately, I never experienced circumstances like this after these abusive sessions ended. I am certain that these experiences helped prevent me from having the dating relationships I desired throughout high school. The feelings of powerlessness, shame, and inadequacy that overcame me during these abusive sessions stayed with me. As it turned out, I never had sexual relations until I was 20 years of age. What happened to LOVE and THE GOLDEN RULE? They were escaping me at this critical time in my life.

My dating experience with Mary and her subsequent tragic death also impacted my growth. It added a new feeling for me: that of guilt. For a long time, I felt I should have been in that car with her and suffered the same consequences. Later, I realized that Mama Kitty's wise decision may have saved my life. This lesson, along with lessons received from therapists later in my life, helped me deal with this. It took a while, but I eventually returned to my mischievous ways and finished high school, scarred from this experience, and many of the others referred to above. I never formally dated again until I was 19 (one time) and then again when I was 21 (after a tour of service in Vietnam). The most important lesson I can learn from this is how Mama Kitty was strong enough to exercise LOVE and THE GOLDEN RULE to save my life, probably.

My education experience in West Virginia was short, full of good and bad situations, and added an obstacle that would influence my life for years to come. This was the introduction of alcoholic beverages. Even though I was asked to resign from the school, I didn't understand the impact that booze had on the outcome. I still had significant self-respect issues and mischievous tendencies, and now, my new friend (booze) has presented itself to me. Booze became my new idol and provided a roadblock to my acceptance of God's First Commandment. My alcoholic behavior blocked my ability to have true feelings for decades to come. I didn't truly LOVE myself and didn't follow THE GOLDEN RULE.

A crucial educational footnote to these events is that five of them had the possibility of directly resulting in my death. The Tarzan, windmill, and urination experiences were most likely safe in that respect. However, they may have added to circumstances leading to my subsequent alcoholism, which eventually impacted my life, leading to circumstances that could have resulted in my death.

An adequate education, with a strong commitment to self-learning, is the foundation of good citizenship. However, all other components of REACTION will also be present in a good citizen. Many of these were cited as relevant to my life experiences referred to earlier in this chapter. Respect, responsibility, acceptance, values, community, truth, and trust were all present in many of these experiences.

As I advanced into adulthood, I was carrying with me several childhood scars that created roadblocks to self-love and my commitment to LOVE and THE GOLDEN RULE. My new friend (booze) also numbed me and further prevented me from accessing vital feelings that could have helped me recognize gaps in my growth.

Let's move on to the next phase in my life.

After working for about 18 months for the Port of New York Authority as a mail clerk, at the age of 19, I volunteered for the draft and became a Private in the U.S. Army in August 1967. Following basic training and advanced individual training, I was sent to Vietnam to train as a communication center specialist. I was based in Da Nang, which was approximately 85 miles from the DMZ. Even though I never was in armed combat, the location of our base (near a large port and airport) was routinely under attack.

My assignment required me to be on a 12/12 rotation, meaning I worked 12 hours and had 12 hours off. The 12 off mainly included playing poker and drinking to the fullest. This lasted for 12 months until I was sent home and honorably released from service in April 1969.

My year in Vietnam became somewhat of a blur. During this time, I received many life (and potentially death) experiences. I grew up a lot during this year. The military taught me several positive life lessons. The most important of which for me were: (1) listening, (2) teamwork, (3) fitness, (4) planning, (5) focus, and, as a result, (6) confidence. These newly acquired lessons initially followed me into civilian life. As time passed, however, the flaws that were present in my character sometimes blocked me from rigidly following these important military lessons. Most importantly, my enhanced dependency on drinking became a greater influence on my behavior.

The summer after I was discharged from the military, I lived at my old home in Virginia. My grandfather had passed on some years earlier. During this time, I developed more confidence and started dating. I also played a lot of golf and softball and spent a great deal of time with my friends. Most of my experiences during this time were fulfilling. However, without my notice, booze was becoming a controlling element in my life.

One other thing happened during this summer that added a significant value to my life. I was accepted as an incoming freshman at Fordham University in New York.

My success in college life had a bumpy start. In my first semester, I failed World History (ironically, a subject that greatly interested me in my later years), resulting in a grade point average of 1.75 for the semester. This caused me to have a forced meeting with the Dean. He got my attention by informing me that the only reason I was accepted at Fordham was that I was a veteran of Vietnam. He further stated that a repeat of this in my second semester would end in my termination from this fine institution. He also strongly suggested that I see a counselor to help me adjust to the rigors of college life further. An important result of this was an aptitude test that prompted me to change my major from marketing to accounting.

This experience with the Dean and the counselor helped me grasp the greater importance of diligently focusing on the educational and moral tools available to me in this Jesuit institution of higher learning.

At the end of this first semester, the most significant event of my life occurred. In one of my classes, I noticed a beautiful young lady. After class, while I was walking to the subway, I saw her again, going in the same direction. I couldn't resist stepping up my pace so I could introduce myself. When we met, I discovered that we were going to take the same subway. We rode together and talked and found an initial fondness for each other. Then I asked her for a date. She accepted. Then, after three years of dating, we were married at St. Patrick's Cathedral in New York City (1973).

This woman became the nucleus of everything good in my life. She was from the Philippines, was Roman Catholic, and was a member of a family that was well respected in her hometown of Cebu. She was not only beautiful but also smart, and she graduated #1 in her class upon graduation. In addition, her value system was strong and well-balanced. She was everything I needed to round out my life. I just knew that God placed her in that Fordham classroom for us to share each other's talents, grow a family, and be valued members of the community.

We were creating a wonderful life for each other. This was enhanced by the birth of our son, Greg, in 1977 and our daughter, Kathy, in 1981. Our love for each other continued to grow, and I am grateful that Nena is by my side today after 50 years of marriage.

Our marriage had some peaks and valleys. I credit the peaks to Nena and the valleys to me. My contribution to the valleys was associated with my other marriage partner (booze). It became clear after 18 years of marriage that I had to do something about this bigamous relationship. As a result, on August 1, 1991, I entered a controlled substance treatment program and never drank alcohol again. I then eliminated the most negative influence on my life, leaving me with an opportunity to make the most of the most positive impact on my life.

I utilized the combined teachings of the treatment program and Alcoholics Anonymous as moral guidelines to follow for self-improvement. One important lesson I took from this was the fact that there is hope. It has always existed around me, and now I can see it. I also learned that I was not alone, which helped me accept I had a problem. Helping others was also an important part of the program. I loved this because I always had a heart filled with charity.

Other important lessons that added strength to my journey were as follows: (1) spend quality time with the right people, (2) the goal is progress and not perfection, (3) prioritize, (4) avoid self-pity, (5) be grateful, and (6) the importance of the Serenity Prayer: "God, grant me the serenity to accept the things I cannot change, the courage to change the things I can, and the wisdom to know the difference."

These teachings eliminated my dependency on a destructive idol (booze) and replaced it with the glorious teachings of God. Eventually, in 1993, I converted from a Southern Baptist to a Roman Catholic and blended my religious faith with that of my wife and her family. This period was the foundation upon which our marriage accelerated into a growth platform that has continued to blossom until today. It prepared us to demonstrate better values for our children and future grand-children to learn from. The community also benefitted from my decision to change careers from Certified Financial Planning to non-profit leadership, which I served for 20 years.

As a result of the key experiences I have described, I finally found myself in a position to be a helpful role model for others. By eliminating booze as an idol, I became able to use the positive values that I was developing to enhance the lives of my family, friends, and the community at large.

I am now able to exercise the values that I have always known to be important. This has led to opportunities for helping others that I could not have imagined. In this chapter, I have touched on many qualities of good citizenship, along with roadblocks to their implementation. Also, above all, tremendous character and strong citizenship can be derived from two simple values: LOVE and THE GOLDEN RULE.

Chapter 5 will delve into things that interfere with a potentially good citizen's ability to continue a path of self-improvement while robbing them of the capability to share and compromise with others positively. On a small scale, these roadblocks to good citizenship could destroy a family or even a community. On a large scale, these could destroy a nation.

Roadblocks To Becoming a Better Citizen

*"Like so many other nations before us, we may succumb
through internal weakness rather than fall before a foreign foe."*
The Conscience of a Conservative
Barry Goldwater

"Stupid people are ruining America."
Herman Cain

*"The good are not willing to rule either for the sake of money or
of honor."*
Plato

Situations can occur whereby citizens spend much of their lives adhering to many or all the REACTION tools described in Chapter 2 and still fall short of being the effective citizens they desire. They may become overwhelmed by the magnitude and depth of the problem they are facing. This could create anxiety and a feeling of depression. They may also see the problem as too complex to understand and, therefore, not pursue a solution. This will cause the citizen to remain ignorant of an issue, resulting in a missed opportunity to make a difference. In addition, the citizen may just tune out and ignore the problem, resulting in a failure of responsibility.

Citizens who make a difference at home or in a community setting will be challenged and eager to get involved, learn more, and tackle their depression. There will be many roadblocks that good citizens may encounter during their journey. I will address many of these in this Chapter.

As I have mentioned, I strongly assert that every citizen is unique and responsible for learning and growing to benefit themselves and others. While these dedicated citizens work ardently on the tools of REACTION, they may be confronted by certain roadblocks that I will describe using another acronym: **"ADAPTS."** I chose ADAPTS because adapting is what is required of a good and conscientious citizen.

The late restauranteur, a fiscally conservative politician and author Herman Cain, described an incident that helped him adapt to a new environment and, at the same time, taught him a valuable life lesson.

> *Mr. Cain, a black man from Georgia, graduated from Morehouse College and moved to a town in Virginia to begin his career as a ballistics analyst with the Department of Navy. Shortly after he arrived, he noticed that he needed a haircut. As a result, he went to a local barbershop where there were two white barbers and one black one. He sat down and began waiting for his turn in the barber's chair. After a long time had passed and other customers had come, been served, and left, he decided to ask the black barber when his turn would come. The barber replied that it wouldn't.*

> *Apparently, in 1967 Virginia, in that town, blacks would not be served in that establishment. With this information, Mr. Cain changed course. He went to a store across the street and bought some clippers. He then trimmed his own hair and did so for years to come.*

Mr. Cain turned a lemon into lemonade by making this decision. He knew he had been confronted with a situation he could not change *(at least by himself at that time)* and developed a Plan B to accomplish his goal of a haircut.

Later in his life, Herman became an acquaintance of mine. As a result of our association, I learned a lot about citizenship. I learned that the haircut lesson is an example of his approach to problem-solving.

He knew that some problems could not immediately be solved. Therefore, the solution should be to ignore the problem until a future opportunity presents itself.

Herman became a successful leader and, for a short time, was the #1 candidate for President of the United States as a member of the Republican Party. His success, as he describes in one of his early books, *Leadership is Common Sense*, came from the values derived from his family, especially his father and grandfather. These positive values were expanded by the education he received at Morehouse College in Atlanta, known as a developer of men. I became aware of the respect and gratitude he had for the valued gifts he received from Morehouse when I asked him for a picture of us together. He responded: absolutely, if we pose alongside the picture of his idol, Benjamin Mays, the President of Morehouse College during Herman's student years.

One of the reasons I referenced Herman Cain is because he sought simple solutions to problems regardless of their complexity. His approach to his haircut problem in Virginia is a refreshing example of finding a solution that (1) solves your immediate concern, (2) bypasses a problem that can't be solved at the time, and (3) makes you aware of a problem that may require your attention in the future.

As a result of Herman's experience, I have described a potential roadblock to good citizenship, which is simple to understand but complex to solve completely. A citizen will face many roadblocks to their growth toward being productive and effective citizens. This doesn't happen overnight. Patience, diligence, and staying on task are required for your desired outcome. Therefore, let's look at how a good citizen **ADAPTS** to roadblocks on their journey of good citizenship. The acronymic headings of **ADAPTS** are defined as follows:

Absence of Knowledge (Ignorance)

Dishonesty (Rule Breaking, Lying, and No Sense of Integrity)

Apathy (Indifference or Detachment)

Party Gridlock (My Way or the Highway)

Tribalism (Communalism)

Self-interest (Ego on Steroids)

<u>**Absence of Knowledge**</u>

As I have already mentioned, learning comes from many sources. To capture the important elements, a commitment to self-learning is required. All the formal education that one can access cannot prepare a person for some unexpected circumstances. Experience, along with formal education, will provide one with a blended set of tools for problem-solving. A lack of knowledge creates a gap in understanding along with an unawareness that results in ignorance.

My children, who are now adults, have always sought knowledge. This is one of the many areas of their growth that I'm most proud of. In fact, my son Greg was coined "Most Knowledgeable" in his Preschool class. Throughout his life (he is 46 at the time of this writing),

Greg has always attempted to seek new information. This includes current and historical data on politics, sports, cooking, health, and much more.

Greg is also confident enough to argue the beliefs derived from his findings with friends and family. These arguments have been designed to not only articulate his position but to learn from opposing viewpoints. He, like many today, avoids arguments with those he doesn't know well.

My daughter, Kathy, also has a strong commitment to learning. Unlike Greg, she stays somewhat current with politics but doesn't seek as much detailed information on that topic as Greg. She also doesn't follow sports, except for University of Georgia football. Greg and the rest of our family live with her obsession with Bulldog football and are happy for her that Georgia won the national championship in each of the past two seasons.

Kathy's knowledge-seeking is mainly in areas that have the potential to improve herself, her family, and her friends. This includes parenting, medical knowledge *(she is a nurse anesthetist),* nutrition, and other areas that add value to her relationships. As an example, during the COVID outbreak, she was our main source of information. This was vital to us especially because her mother *(my wife, of course)* has a chronic condition that, if targeted by COVID, could produce negative results.

My wife, Nena, is also an extremely knowledgeable person. I will not embarrass her with examples in this book. She is a very private person. I will say this about her, however. I have learned more lessons, as an adult, that have added value to my growth from her than anyone else I have known.

Nena, Greg, and Kathy have been instrumental in providing loving additions to my inventory of knowledge, resulting in valuable tools for enhancing success on my journey to becoming a better citizen.

Key to this Absence of Knowledge roadblock in becoming a good citizen that we all face today is *where* we acquire our information. It comes at us fast and furious. It's non-stop. Some information is based on truth with a desire to be helpful. Some are based on lies or deception and seek to taint our knowledge. Examples are social media, the internet, cable news, blogs, etc. I honestly believe this never-ending blast of information is too much for our brains to digest constructively.

This is where I would like to explain the difference between ignorance and stupidity. Ignorance is simply a lack of knowledge. Stupidity is a lack of intelligence. The acquisition of knowledge can reduce ignorance, whereas a stupid person may require remedial help to understand an issue. In addition, some stupid people just refuse to learn or may be too lazy to search for knowledge.

I mentioned in Chapter 2 that one important aspect of becoming a good citizen is to vote. A stupid person who does not stay informed of the needs of their fellow man or is locked into a one-sided opinion of an issue without an attempt to see an opposing viewpoint is not following good citizenship. On the other hand, a person who seeks new knowledge and understands both sides of an issue is on the road toward good citizenship.

Late in my non-profit career, I acted as Executive Director for The Glenn Pelham Foundation. This Foundation was a brainchild of Melissa Wade, who was an Emory University professor and once earned notoriety as one of the top collegiate debaters in the United States. She was truly the CEO, President, Debate Leader, and Chief Bottle Washer (ha ha) of the Foundation. She basically did it all. I was there simply to lead in the development of a strategic plan and to act as a fundraiser.

The Foundation's function was to teach urban middle and high school students the value of debate. They did this through relevant national and global topics that were in the news at the time. The skills that these students developed were extraordinary. They learned to argue both sides of an issue, giving them a depth of knowledge of the issue. The process not only enhanced their knowledge but also improved their grades gave them self-respect, and, yes, put them on a solid path toward good citizenship.

Effective voting requires the proper use of a citizen's knowledge. If adequate knowledge is lacking because it isn't sought or is blocked by outside sources, the result will be an uninformed or ignorant person voting for people and things that have the potential to change their lives and the lives of their neighbors for years to come. For all people to have a chance to be free and pursue their idea of happiness, a knowledgeable commitment to voting is mandatory. When we think about the importance of voting, we should remember that the Constitution has provided the laws necessary for free citizens to exercise their rights, and the Declaration of Independence is the moral foundation of the Constitution. The election of a servant-hearted, moral person who is knowledgeable of the role of the office sought should be the desired goal of the citizen voter. This cannot effectively happen if the voter doesn't acquire the necessary knowledge about the candidate's qualifications. What is worse is when the voter stupidly allows outside noise *(biased blogs, cable news, etc.)* to influence their vote. These outside sources usually have an agenda and require diligent vetting before they can be relied on.

To summarize the importance of knowledge to become a valuable citizen, I will quote key parts of The Declaration of Independence:

> ***"…a decent respect to the opinions of mankind requires that they should declare the causes which impel them to separation.***
>
> ***We hold these truths to be self-evident that all men are created equal, that they are endowed by their Creator with certain unalienable Rights, that among these are Life, Liberty, and the pursuit of Happiness."***

Skipping to the last sentence…

"And for the support of this Declaration, with a firm reliance on the protection of divine Providence, we mutually pledge to each other our Lives, our Fortunes, and our sacred Honor."

<u>Dishonesty</u>

"Honesty" is such a lonely word.

Everyone is so untrue.

Honesty is hardly ever heard.

And mostly what I need from you.

Billy Joel

Chorus of his hit song, "Honesty" 1978

The lyrics from this popular song are a proper starting point for delving into the important topic of honesty. I see honesty as an example of moral correctness. It leads to integrity *(honesty combined with moral principles)*. The military likes to use the word "honor" as an expectation of the character of a soldier.

It appears to me that Billy Joel was becoming cynical as he apparently saw the practice of honesty slipping away from many when he wrote this song. He sensed, however, that without it, a healthy relationship cannot effectively grow. This hasn't changed today. Many people go cowardly through life without letting others know who they really are. This creates a significant gap in their relationships, which may result in the end of what could have been good friendships. If a little risk is taken, with honesty, candor, and understanding, much can be accomplished toward the growth of two citizens.

I would like to share a personal story that had a tremendous impact on me and several others.

In the early 2000s, while I was Chief Financial Officer for the Boys & Girls Clubs of Metro Atlanta, I was charged with leading the organization's operations staff in a workshop. Participants included the key management of our 20-plus clubs along with the Regional Vice Presidents (approximately 60 staff members).

An hour or so into the morning of the session, I noticed that many folks were not paying attention. To encourage listening and participation, I decided to gamble on a new approach. I turned off the overhead projector and abandoned my original agenda.

I knew that most of the audience had pre-conceived ideas of who I was, along with a perception of what my motives might be. I was seen by many as an ivory tower bureaucrat who probably couldn't understand them well enough to provide them with any productive level of leadership.

Then, I took the big step of telling them my life story. I started by letting them know that I saw our biggest barrier to effectively working together was a lack of trust. To tackle that barrier, I emotionally told them my life story.

I wanted them to understand that we were not that different. Even though we came from different cultural backgrounds, we shared the desire to be respected and equipped with the tools required for personal growth and for the organization. Before this could happen, they needed to know me intimately.

My story lasted over an hour. I gave them the good, bad, and ugly of my life. Finally, they were listening with the looks that seemed to say, "Who is this guy?"

One part of my story related to my relationship with Mama Kitty. She loved baseball and was a big fan of Dizzy Dean, a pitcher for the Chicago Cubs and St. Louis Cardinals in the 1930s and early 1940s. Dizzy was an excellent pitcher and played a key role in the Cardinals winning the World Series in 1934. He was the winning pitcher in two of their four wins. In 1953, he was elected to the Baseball Hall of Fame.

I believe that the thing Mama Kitty most liked about Dizzy was that he was truly himself. What you see is what you get. After retirement from baseball, he became an announcer for CBS's and NBC's *Game of the Week*. Dizzy was basically undereducated; however, he was loved by his audiences when he mispronounced players' names and used his own version of grammar. He would say things like that batter really "slud" into second base. He was also self-deprecating. One of his quotes was, "The doctors x-rayed my head and found nothing." And another, "The good Lord was good to me. He gave me a strong body, a good right arm, and a weak mind."

Well, one Saturday, while Mama Kitty and I were visiting her brother in Philadelphia, who lived close to Connie Mack Stadium, the home of the Phillies, we got tickets to the game. Lo and behold, it was the televised *Game of the Week*, and Dizzy Dean was broadcasting. Before the game, he was walking down a nearby aisle, and Mama Kitty urged me to get his autograph. I was 9 or 10 years old then, with all shyness and a lack of self-respect, so I told her I wouldn't. From that day on, I felt I let my grandmother, who gave me so much, down. When Mama Kitty died in the early 1980s, one of the main things I remembered about our relationship was how I let her down by not getting Dizzy Dean's autograph.

This story brought tears to my eyes and many others in the audience. As I went on to tell the rest of my story, lunchtime approached. During lunch, I received many accolades for doing what I did and was told by many that the glass shield had been broken and that they were ready to go to work with my guidance.

This workshop led to all of us working together ardently to create our next strategic plan. It also helped me work on key organizational issues, including improvement in benefits and the development of sound budgets.

The most rewarding gift I received from this experience came a couple of weeks later when I noticed a package on my desk. I opened it and found a card signed by the attendees thanking me for what I did. To my pleasant surprise, also in the box was a caricature of Dizzy Dean with his autograph. The cycle was now complete, and I could hang this thoughtful gift alongside a photo of Mama Kitty. The two still hang together in my room today.

One other special gift I received because of this workshop came from one of the attendees, Debra. Debra moved to Atlanta after Hurricane Katrina destroyed her home. I only knew Debra for a short time, but during that time, I found her to be a hard worker with a strong faith in God. She wrote me a note a couple of weeks later. The following is her note.

John,

What you did in the workshop on Friday, May 12, 2006, is difficult to put into words. Your commitment and investment spoke volumes. Your invitation to be part of a team opened many emotions in me. You were honest, open, and naked before all of us.

I know you are not a perfect man, and you probably think you missed the mark. You have not missed the mark; you've hit the target. Organizations change for the better when leaders (heads) are willing to expose their humanness before others. You took a risk that was

beyond yourself. It will forever have an impact on me and others.

You took courage in the arena where few are willing to tread. I guarantee that good change will occur because of your courage. Thanks for allowing me to be a part of it. I don't exactly know where I fit, but in the meantime, I will give my all to support the vision.

Debra went on to share the following:

John Hurlbut

"A Man Willing to be Naked"

I know God loves you a great deal.

You are honest, and you are real.
You stood "naked" before us, and now
Boys & Girls Club of Metro Atlanta has a chance to heal.

You prepared to receive each and every one of us.
You exposed yourself and allowed us to build trust.
Working together is not an option but a must.

You shared the vision in your heart.
You let us know we have a part.
It is a new beginning and a fresh start.

Your willingness to be "naked" and exposed did open many a door.
Now, we can go forward, and as a team, we will soar.

Jesus' favorite child
Outstanding mentor
Honest and real
Noble leader

Honorable and humble hero
Uniquely and wonderfully made
Risk taker
Loving and caring
Burdened for the underprivileged
Ultimate leader
Trustworthy

A "Silver" Friend
Debra

I don't have the words to describe the impact that these gifts had on me. They helped me turn a page in my life and place before me an opportunity to be a better person. As I commit to continued growth toward being a better person, I will be more capable of positively influencing others and feeding nourishment to a healthier society.

Billy Joel was right. Honesty can be a lonely word, but it doesn't have to be. It is mostly what we need from each other.

Apathy

An Oxford definition of apathy is a lack of interest, enthusiasm, or concern. I will further add the synonyms indifference and detachment. An apathetic feeling may be associated with a potentially serious condition of depression, which may require psychological assistance. Accordingly, I see apathy as a less medically dangerous condition than depression with the capability, however, of growing into a serious medical concern.

Don't misunderstand me. Apathy can be a major roadblock to becoming a happy and productive citizen. Apathetic people lose their interest in things that used to be important to them. Apathy can affect one's ability to make decisions, set goals, perform well at work, engage in healthy activities, form and maintain friendships, and basically become numb to their surroundings. Essentially, apathy reduces a person's ability to enjoy life.

It is obviously difficult for an individual with apathy to perform many of the duties of a good citizen. Some of these are focusing on learning, accepting responsibility, paying attention to their health, being industrious, and following important community obligations such as voting. These stand right in the face of a citizen acting diligently on reaction.

An apathetic feeling will remain until a person makes important changes in their life. Before I go further on this topic, I must present a caveat that I am not a doctor or psychotherapist.

A serious case of apathy *(anxiety, depression, etc.)* may require professional treatment and medication. However, an advancing milder form can be addressed through lifestyle changes and the support of family, friends, and even co-workers. Some ideas to counter apathy are:

- Be sociable. Isolation negatively affects the mind.
- Go to a new restaurant.
- Focus on gratitude.
- Exercise or just take a walk in a new environment.
- Focus on better nutrition.
- Accept that you have a problem.
- Be confident that your condition is temporary.
- As you see a change, learn from your past condition.
- Pray.

I have experienced apathy, anxiety, and depression at different times during my life. As a result, I can tell you that each time, my ability to feel useful and perform effectively at work or useful to family and friends was seriously impaired.

The first time it happened was in 1991. At that time, my feeling of hopelessness led me to a treatment center where I first accepted my problem with alcoholism. Through this treatment, I learned a great deal about coping with the disease of alcoholism and was introduced to many ideas on how to replace my bad habits with good ones. I also learned how my bad habits negatively affected others. This reality hurt me deeply. I always wanted to improve the lives of others and to be a good role model for them to follow.

During my six weeks in treatment, along with two years of Alcoholics Anonymous, I stopped drinking, developed a greater relationship with God, and began replacing my bad habits with new ones that were healthier for me and those around me.

After I finished treatment, I put aside my career as a Certified Financial Planner and started one with the Boys & Girls Clubs of Metro Atlanta. I felt comfortable with this because I cared about the growth of kids and felt it gave me purpose. A couple of years after I was hired, I was promoted to Vice President of Finance. This position in senior management provided me with the opportunity to collaborate with other dedicated leaders to create much positive change that allowed the kids we served to have more tools to enhance their growth.

Subsequently, less than two years after the retreat, where I shared my life story, something started happening. An outside force was attacking me and producing a feeling of uselessness. I didn't really understand it, but I knew I had to make a change. Somehow, I felt there was an imminent force that could impede my ability to impact the future growth of the organization I loved. I had to leave, so I resigned in 2007.

After I resigned, my feeling of uselessness stayed with me for almost a year. During this time, I accepted a position as Chief Financial

Officer with another non-profit organization. My activities in this position did nothing to improve my apathy. I just couldn't perform and resigned after nine months.

Subsequently, I took a position with TAG Education Collaborative (TAG Ed), the 501c foundation of the Technology Association of Georgia (TAG), that promoted STEM (science, technology, engineering, and math) education. This excited me because I loved mathematics and embraced the importance of science, technology, and engineering. My title was Executive Director; however, I was more of a chief operating officer since the President of TAG was the Chief Executive Officer, and I reported to him.

One of my responsibilities was to build a Board of Directors for TAG Ed. I then recruited a professor of mathematics from Georgia Tech, prominent technology leaders, and several successful entrepreneurs who were interested in enhancing the ability of students to make a difference in the growing world of technological advancements. We formed an effective team that introduced programs that provided access to high school and college students to display their creativity.

For a couple of years, I was excited about our accomplishments. Once again, however, an apathetic feeling was taking over me. The desire to be alone once again prevailed, and I resigned.

A year later, I began a three-year journey with The Glenn Pelham Foundation, an organization I mentioned earlier in this chapter. With the leadership of Mrs. Wade, I was able to build a board of directors, create a strategic plan, and introduce activities that enhanced fundraising. Again, something was missing in my life that affected my job performance. As a result, I left the organization and retired in 2014.

What was missing in all the experiences I referred to? The answer, I believe, is I wasn't finished with developing myself. The tools I learned and developed early in my period of treatment for alcohol abuse were somewhat dormant in my daily life. I didn't respect myself or faithfully trust myself or others. I needed to accept who I am and discover the purpose for the last act of my life.

I have been retired for nine years now. In 2014, my final journey began with gratitude. I accepted and was grateful that I was a child of God and I was loved and respected by those close to me. This included Nena, Greg, Kathy, and eventually Kathy's husband and two children. I also had a small group of close friends whom I trusted to be candid with me if I didn't seem to be acting functionally. Now, I entered a period where I could grow without outside pressure.

I then listed an inventory of gaps in my life that impacted my ability to be a better citizen. Some of these are:

1. Early childhood abandonment
2. Dysfunction in my early family life
3. Poor self-esteem ("I am just not good enough")
4. Dishonesty with myself
5. Lack of respect for myself
6. Shielding who I am from others
7. Failure to improve my knowledge
8. Avoiding proper exercise and nutrition
9. Failing to fulfill all my job responsibilities
10. Bombarded by political dysfunction
11. Lack of balance in my life
12. Without goals
13. Not focusing on priorities
14. Absence of purpose

All these inventory items work to create apathy. I am proud to say that I have made tremendous progress in the past nine years. I am confident that I have improved myself in all the defects of character I have mentioned. I haven't conquered them, but I have made progress in understanding and dealing with them. In some cases, I accepted the things that happened and understood I couldn't change them. Then, I studied what I could learn from them. In some cases, I had to improve

my attitude, set goals, be more open, prioritize, and, as a result, change
the things I can.

One thing I always must remember is improvement is derived from consistent progress and not the desire to be perfect.

This focus on progress and not perfection helped me tremendously. The outside pressure is off. I feel I am now free to pursue the gifts that life has provided me. I can also feel more qualified to be a role model for those who depend on me. I am no longer held back by apathy, anxiety, or depression.

One final thought: I believe that anyone who believes in their Higher Power embraces a feeling of gratitude and accepts that they can reduce apathy and embark on a road toward becoming a productive citizen.

Party Gridlock

In 2023 politics, political leaders operate in the direction of their Parties. They utilize a firm handshake, velvet tongue, and engaging smile to connect them with potential voters initially. But really, who are they? Do they have adequate knowledge of the job they are seeking? Do they have integrity and exercise good judgment? Most of the answers to these questions will be missing when we vote if we don't take a deeper dive into the candidates' backgrounds.

Another issue that may impact a person's ability to know the candidate better is the power behind Party politics. The Party will determine whether the candidate has what the Party desires to disseminate the Party's message. This has been going on for decades. The problem with this today is that the two major Parties *(Republican and Democrat)* are so controlled by party factions that there is no room for honest debate on the critical issues facing citizens. This creates a divide that grows without creative compromise.

Our Founding Fathers had the insight to see this eventuality. There was no mention of political parties in The Constitution. James Madison, who worked with John Jay and Alexander Hamilton on The Federalist Papers, wrote in Federalist 10 that one of the functions of a "well-constructed" Union should be "its tendency to break and control the violence of faction."

Today, factions are more powerful than ever. They are controlled by Political Action Committees, big-money lobbyists, large special interest groups, and even radical extremists.

Our first US President, George Washington, was the only President to run for office without allegiance to a political party. After he took office, he was referred to as a Federalist since that party was pro-Constitution. In Washington's farewell address in 1796, he cited the following about parties:

> *"The spirit of party serves always to distract the public counsels and enfeeble the public administration. It agitates the community with ill-founded jealousies and false alarms, kindles the animosity of one part against another, foments occasional riot and insurrection."*

Until he died in 1799, Washington believed we would eventually eliminate the party system. His belief proved wrong, however, since every US President after him campaigned as part of a political party. Seven different Parties have endorsed the Presidents after Washington. They were Federalist, Democratic-Republican, Democrat, Whig, Republican, National Union, and possibly The Know Nothing Party of Millard Fillmore, although he was referred to as a Whig. Since 1869, every President has been a member of either the Republican or Democratic Party.

Big money entities like corporations invest in both Parties, making sure they get something from the winner. Special interest groups, or factions, lobby the President and Congress, and their Party leaders constantly. Billionaires are controlling factions within both Parties. Examples would be George Soros, who supports Democratic causes, and hedge fund tycoon Ken Griffin, who supports Republican causes.

The Parties have changed their focus many times over the years when doing so provides them with a better chance to attract voters. If you look at history, the Democratic Party of the 1950s is more like the Republican Party today.

All these things have evolved from the top down. The power of biased media and sophisticated political campaigns facilitated by first-class marketing programs result in the average citizen being brainwashed. Herman Cain, in his book *They Think You're Stupid*, coined a term that is becoming more and more relevant today. It was *"politically homeless,"* describing a lost citizen without a political party to rely on.

What do we do as good citizens to counteract this growing political gridlock? I will address this in Chapter 6. For now, acquiring as much knowledge as possible on how we got here in the first place is paramount. An ignorance of history is more of an enemy to us today than ever before. A paragraph from Jon Meacham's book, *The Soul of America*, describes how important knowledge of history is today.

The past and the present tell us that demagogues can only thrive when a substantial portion of the demos – the people – want them to. In The American Commonwealth (1889), James Bryce warned of the dangers of a renegade president. Bryce's view was not that the individual himself, from the White House, could overthrow the Constitution. Disaster would come, Bryce believed, at the hands of a demagogic president with an enthusiastic public base. "A bold President who knew himself to be supported by a majority in the country might be tempted to override the law and deprive the minority of the protection which the law provides it." Bryce wrote.

"He might be a tyrant, not against the masses, but with the masses." The cheering news is that hope is not lost. "The people have often made mistakes," Harry Truman said, "but given time and the facts, they will make the corrections."

Today's party gridlock creates group thinking that impedes an individual's ability to participate effectively in decisions that relate to their well-being. They become controlled by factions who don't communicate, don't respect each other, and, with the help of biased media, hate each other. This results in no ability for the factions to compromise. This *"my way or the highway"* attitude prevents our leaders from working together to properly lead us on a path toward our pursuit of happiness. The concerned citizen fades away into their "politically homeless" arena with a feeling that there is no hope.

Tribalism

An adjunct to Party Gridlock is tribalism or communalism. For this book, tribalism is where people are overly loyal to their group. When their group digs in and becomes motivated by extremism, their motives become solidified, and the potential of class warfare develops. Jon Meacham referred to Jane Addams, a 19th and 20th-century activist and a co-founder of The American Civil Liberties Union. She wrote: "We know instinctively that if we grow contemptuous of our fellows and consciously limit our intercourse to certain kinds of people whom we have previously decided to respect, we not only tremendously circumscribe our range of life, but limit the scope of ethics."

In my own words, mass tribes equipped with their motives at the expense of others are not only ignorant of the moral message of The Declaration of Independence, but they also demonstrate a total disregard for those who may have useful motives of their own.

Yuval Levin, in *A Time to Build,* referenced the work of Robert Nisbet in *Twilight of Authority.* In this 2000 book, originally published in 1975, Nisbet wrote: "American adults have fewer close friends, spend less time with others, and feel more disconnected today than they did a generation or two ago. And although it is easier than ever to be exposed to and informed by a wide range of views, Americans increasingly live in cultural and political bubbles, hearing only affirmations and elucidations of what they already believe."

My life has been impacted by tribalism. I have found myself polarized and lonely as a result. My core self is being lost. Accordingly, I have not been faithful to who I really am or desire to be. I am attempting to participate in life without true LOVE for myself and not adhering to THE GOLDEN RULE as it should relate to me. In essence, *I do unto me as I wouldn't want anyone else to do to me.* In addition, I knew that if I truly loved myself, I had to correct the control that elements of tribalism had on my life.

Where did this start for me? How did I become a member of a tribe? Most of these reasons have been mentioned in the listing inventory of gaps in my life that I referred to earlier. I was somewhat lost and without a purpose. I was so lost that I began trusting questionable sources of information. I was convincing myself that I was a political conservative when I saw myself as a fiscal conservative with side beliefs commensurate with social policies. I found that I am not a perfect fit in today's Republican or Democratic parties. Those parties don't even know what they really stand for.

In my opinion, America's political parties today are comprised of members who have forgotten that the heart of America is their people, who they are ignoring in the sense that all of America's people have the right to be treated equally and have the freedom to pursue their idea of happiness. As a result, it seems to me that America's leaders are controlled by "tribes" of all kinds and will sacrifice who they are to please these entities to support their re-election. RE-ELECTION FIRST, PEOPLE SECOND is their unspoken motto.

Unknowingly, a major tribe that was influencing me was Fox News, the self-proclaimed *"fair and balanced"* network. For the better part of two decades, I watched Fox News almost exclusively for information. It took me until 2017 to realize that something was wrong with this.

I voted for Donald Trump in 2016 basically because I felt a businessman would result in favorable changes in Washington. This opinion, along with rhetoric from Fox News, brainwashed me that Hillary Clinton is corrupt, cares only about herself, and has no business in the White House.

In the first year of his Presidency, Trump signed some Executive Orders and led the passage of some legislation that pleased me. However, in 2017, he started revealing who he might be. His *very fine people on both sides"* comment regarding violence in Charlottesville endorsed hatred over love. Many felt that his comments supported white nationalists over counter-protesters. This instance, along with Fox News' unabashed support of Trump's comments, had a lasting effect on me.

I started to see President Trump differently and released myself from the shackles of Fox News. From the Charlottesville incident until today, I have not watched Fox News for serious information. Their agenda is based on things that I don't understand, and my gut tells me to stop watching.

In 2020, I voted for Joe Biden to be president. Even though I didn't believe in many of his policies, I felt more people with integrity controlled him than Donald Trump. As a side, Donald Trump has revealed more of who he really is after the 2020 election. He has shown that he is controlled by a tribe of dangerous people who want to destroy our democracy, not to mention his own egoism.

Since I have rid myself of a tribe that was brainwashing me, I have experienced a wonderful feeling of freedom. The Serenity Prayer, along with more balance and purpose in my life, has made me less dependent on tribes to influence who I am.

In the words of Don Santo: *"The issue of tribalism, racism, segregation of whichever form and manner it beholds, and separatist arguments…All these are toxic elements in our living as a people."*

<u>Self-Interest</u>

A definition of self-interest is: *"one's personal interest or advantage, especially when pursued without regard for others."*

Self-interest is a good attribute at its core. One may have a self-interest in learning to acquire better knowledge for oneself. One may have a self-interest in seeking a job that pays more to be able to support a growing family better. However, self-interest, without an awareness of its effect on others, can lead to non-altruistic means and goals. This type of self-interest often leads to decay in society.

This component of **ADAPTS** focuses on the negative aspect of self-interest, which I describe as *"ego on steroids."* When self-interest becomes ego-driven with the desire to prove oneself greater than others, a breakdown in societal connection is introduced. If this ego is fed, one's self-interest gravitates toward a feeling of superiority. Morally, no human being is superior to or worth more than another. However, people are different in the sense that they have unique skills. When the holder sees one's differences as superior to those of others, the negative effects of the ego take over.

In my opinion, this is what happened to one of the most dangerous tyrants of the 20th century, Adolf Hitler. It is common knowledge that Hitler's father saw him as frail and sickly during his childhood. His father's disappointment in him grew and resulted in his abuse of his son. This lack of fatherly love, as Hitler saw it, wounded him and had an extremely negative impact on his self-worth. This period of his life created a personality disorder that Hitler carried with him to his grave.

As Hitler grew, this personality disorder matured, resulting in resentment and envy for others. He sought "superiority" to counteract his feelings of "inferiority." His ambition, coupled with this superiority complex, put him on a path of destruction as he acquired a mass following. His ego was now on steroids. He saw himself as the only person capable of creating the perfect world. Unfortunately, this would come at the expense of those he now saw as inferior, those he defined as inadequate to be members of his "master race."

Hitler's eventual leadership *(autocracy)* was based on hatred, resentment, and racism. Even though he felt he didn't really measure up, he convinced masses of Germans that he was the special one ordained to change the world for the better. According to Henry Murray, former Director of the Harvard Psychological Clinic, "Often gifted with the ability to influence and motivate masses through the power of oration and messianic vision, such leaders become the incarnation of the crowd's unspoken needs and cravings. At the same time, much like the mythic figures of the Antichrist in Christianity, Armilus in Judaism, and Masih ad-Dajjal in Islam, they are not merely false prophets, but, even more perniciously, the embodiment of evil."

Hitler is an example of ego on steroids. We must use this example to learn that no one person is superior to others. If that person has an agenda that is only known to them and convinces others that only they can lead the world into a new order in God's spirit, we will be on the road to destruction.

Revisiting my analogy that cells in the human body are like citizens of the world, I believe that improper cell growth can create problems for the entire body. I see this as an example of the effects of a Hitler figure on mankind.

I will cite Scitable, a reference library comprised of a worldwide community of scientists, researchers, teachers, and students, to further explain my assumption that *"Cancer is unchecked cell growth."* According to Scitable:

> ***"Mutations in genes can cause cancer by accelerating cell division rates or inhibiting normal controls on***

the system, such as cell cycle arrest or programmed cell death. As a mass of cancerous cells grows, it can develop into a tumor. Cancer cells can also invade neighboring tissues and sometimes even break off and travel to other parts of the body, leading to the formation of new tumors at these sites."

Do tumors resemble a person like Hitler? I believe so.

Do tumors resemble any national or international figure today? I believe so.

Unchecked, ego-centered self-interest can develop into a global tumor capable of destroying the ability of all people to act as valuable members of a society with respect for all. Unfortunately, this *"global tumor"* has occurred at different times in the world and has had the potential to destroy the lives that we most desire. Why?

In the words of John Steinbeck: *"It has always seemed strange to me that… the things we admire in men, kindness and generosity, openness, honesty, understanding, and feeling, are the concomitants of failure in our system. And those traits we detest, sharpness, greed, acquisitiveness, meanness, egotism, and self-interest, are the traits of success. And while men admire the quality of the first, they love the produce of the second."*

Steinbeck answered the question of why *People allow it to happen.* The road to becoming good citizens demands that we will not allow a civilization tumor to destroy our lives. We must focus ardently on the elements of **REACTION** to provide us with the tools to become the citizens that we need to be. If not, we will risk losing a sense of who we desire to be. That is citizens with LOVE in their hearts and those who practice THE GOLDEN RULE in all their activities.

Franklin D. Roosevelt masterfully stated: "Virtues are lost in self-interest as rivers are lost in the sea."

A quote by the Dalai Lama further expresses my feelings regarding self-interest.

> *"We are driven by self-interest; it is necessary to survive. But we need wise self-interest that is generous and cooperative, taking other's interests into account. Cooperation comes from friendship, friendship comes from trust, and trust comes from kind-heartedness. Once you have a genuine sense of concern for others, there is no room for cheating, bullying, or exploitation."*

In summary, as we begin to apply **REACTION** to our approach toward good citizenship, we may encounter certain roadblocks that can end our journey. But we don't have to allow that to happen. We have now introduced the most prominent of these roadblocks through the acronym **ADAPTS**. Addressing these barriers head-on is among the demands of becoming a good citizen.

Again, the solution is rooted in the twin virtues of LOVE and THE GOLDEN RULE.

Chapter Six

21st Century Issues

"The great paradox of the 21st century is that, in this age of powerful technology, the biggest problems we face internationally are problems of the human soul."
Ralph Peters

"The only skill that will be important in the 21st century is the skill of learning new skills. Everything else will become obsolete over time."
Peter Drucker

"We need an independent media to hold people like me to account."
George H. W. Bush

"It's time to fundamentally change the way we do business in Washington. To help build a new foundation for the 21st century, we need to reform our government so that it is more efficient, more transparent, and more creative. That will demand more thinking and a new sense of responsibility for every dollar that is spent."
Barack Obama

"We are bound by ideals that teach us what it means to be citizens. Every child must be taught these ideals. Every citizen

*must uphold them... I ask you to be citizens. Citizens, not
spectators. Citizens, not subjects. Responsible citizens building
communities of service and a nation of character."*
George W. Bush

So far, we have explored the qualities of a good citizen and the
roadblocks a good citizen may encounter on their journey. Today, we
are two-plus decades into the 21st century. During this short time, we
have experienced several events that are beginning to impact American
lives in a major way. Some of the most significant of these are:

1.   September 11, 2001
2.   2002 invasion of Afghanistan
3.   2003 invasion of Iraq
4.   Facebook was formed.
5.   2004 legalization of same-sex marriage in Massachusetts
6.   2004 landing on Mars
7.   YouTube was founded.
8.   Hurricane Katrina in 2005
9.   Twitter was launched.
10. Spotify was launched.
11. 2006 execution of Saddam Hussein
12. 2007 introduction of the iPhone
13. The sub-prime crisis triggered the 2007 global recession
14. Barack Obama was elected President in 2008.
15. Google Chrome was released.
16. The Tesla Roadster was introduced in 2008.
17. Bitcoin was launched in 2009.
18. The iPad was introduced in 2010.
19. Instagram was launched in 2010.
20. Osama Bin Laden was shot dead in Pakistan in 2011.
21. The world population reached 7 billion in 2011.
22. Snapchat was launched in 2011.

23. The Iraq war ended in 2011.

24. Supreme Court approved same-sex marriage in 2015.

25. Juno entered orbit in Jupiter in 2016.

26. Mother Teresa was canonized by Pope Francis in 2016.

27. The Paris Agreement (global warming) was signed by 195 nations in 2016.

28. Pokémon Go was released.

29. U.S. troops withdrew from Afghanistan after 15 years in 2016.

30. TikTok was launched.

31. Donald Trump was elected President in 2016.

32. James Khashoggi was assassinated inside the Saudi consulate in 2018.

33. The China/United States trade war began in 2018.

34. Donald Trump was impeached in 2019.

35. George Floyd was murdered in 2020.

36. COVID-19 spread worldwide in 2020.

37. Joe Biden was elected President in 2020.

38. On 1/6/21, supporters of Donald Trump attacked the U.S. Capitol.

39. Donald Trump was impeached for the second time in 2021.

40. Russia began a military buildup in Ukraine in 2021.

41. Russia invaded Ukraine in 2022.

42. Elizabeth II died in 2022 and was replaced by Charles III.

43. "Hamas' brutal attack on Israel.

I see this list as significant events that affected people worldwide. You may notice that several of these are technological advancements, many of which have drastically changed how we send and receive information. In addition to these, several themes developed in the early part of this century.

- Gun violence (especially in schools) has accelerated.
- Climate and weather-related disasters are surging.
- Middle East tensions remain prevalent and relevant.

- Vladimir Putin has been elected President four times (exceeding Russia's two-term Constitutional limit).

Certainly, there have been other events in the first part of the 21st century that could be included. However, I hope to cover those themes as I move into the major issues that I see confronting mankind in the remainder of the 21st century. As I have demonstrated earlier, I like acronyms to describe my assertions broadly. Accordingly, in this chapter, I will use the acronym FACING CHANGE as a title for the major 21st-century issues that I see as most important. Let's look at these.

Food Security

Attack on Democracy at home

Crime and racism

Immigration

National debt and deficit

Grip that Media holds on our lives!

Climate change and global warming

Health concerns

Artificial intelligence

Nuclear war concerns

Global tensions

Education

As you can see, I have education last on the list. However, it is far from the least important, and without it, none of the 21st century's issues can be effectively addressed. Before I go any further, I would like to share a quote that may help explain the heart of our problem with American decision-making.

"All people are born alike – except for Republicans and Democrats."

Groucho Marx

<u>Food Security</u>

Is food security really a problem for this century? Isn't there enough food worldwide to feed everyone in the world? Can't improved technology solve any food imbalance? Well…maybe not!

According to the World Economic Forum on November 23, 2020:

- By 2050, there will be 2 million more people on Earth than at that time.
- Today's agriculture can't deliver enough food to meet the need.
- So, change is needed to increase the output across the globe.
- But it mustn't be done at the expense of an increasingly fragile environment.
- And the world's most undernourished need help now.

The WEF went on to say that the demand for food in 2050 will be 56% greater than in 2010.

In this report, the WEF cited five reasons why food security is a major issue in the 21st century.

1. Population growth

2. Changing tastes. As people become more affluent, they start eating foods that are richer in processed foods, meat, and dairy. But to produce more meat requires growing more grain.

3. Climate change. Currently, 40% of the world's landmass is arid, and rising temperatures will turn more of it into desert.

4. Water scarcity. 28% of agriculture lies in water-stressed regions.

5. Troubled farmers. Fewer people are choosing farming as an occupation. Meanwhile, global food prices are rising, arable land continues to be lost to urban sprawl, and soil is being degraded by over-farming.

The WEF further explains what makes ensuring food security so complex. They use India as an example. "Agriculture accounts for 18% of the economy's output and 41% of its workforce. Yet, according to the Food and Agriculture Organization (FAO) of the United Nations, some 189 million Indians are undernourished. This represents the largest number of hungry people in a single country. An estimated 14% of the population of India are too malnourished to lead a normal life."

By the way, 14% who are too malnourished to lead a normal life are equivalent, roughly, to 60% of the population of the United States.

Also, it isn't just India. Other regions of the world, such as Sub-Saharan Africa, the Caribbean, Western Asia, Central America, South America, and Northern Africa, have severe problems with nutrition.

Sadly, it is not just a problem beyond our borders. For the last decade or so, approximately 2.5% of Americans have been undernourished. Since my wife is Filipino and has her family there, I will add that the Philippines has a malnutrition rate greater than 5%.

Having enough to eat is a basic human need. The share of undernourished people is a leading indicator for food security and nutrition used by the FAO. A significant result of undernourishment is indicated among mothers and children, where it is a leading risk factor for death and poor health.

A question American citizens must ask is:

With our wealth of resources, public and private, how can we allow 2.5% of our population to be undernourished?

Attack on Democracy at Home

America's democracy is under attack whether we accept it or not. The authoritarian "playbook" has been established in many countries around the world. Suppose a person with authoritarian tendencies gains control and convinces the masses that they are the only person to lead our country. In that case, we will be experiencing the first steps in losing the rights provided to us by the Declaration of Independence. We will be on the verge of losing our freedom.

This has happened in several countries in the past 35 years. For example, populist outsiders have taken power in four Latin American countries (Bolivia, Ecuador, Peru, and Venezuela), resulting in weakened democracies.

In *How Democracies Die*, Steven Levitsky and Daniel Ziblatt take a deep dive into the reasons democracies have failed in the past. Many examples of leaders who were successful in transforming a democracy into an autocracy are cited. These include Hitler, Mussolini, Fujimori, Chavez, and others. Their work goes further and describes the characteristics of authoritarian behavior. To do this, they used the work of Juan Linz, a political scientist who was born in Weimar, Germany, and raised during Spain's civil war. Building on the work of Linz, Levitsky and Ziblatt developed the following "Four Key Indicators of Authoritarian Behavior."

1. Rejection of (or weak commitment to) democratic rules of the game

- Do they reject the Constitution or express a willingness to violate it?

- Do they express a need for antidemocratic measures, such as canceling elections, violating or suspending the Constitution, banning certain organizations, or restricting basic civil or political rights?

- Do they seek to use (or endorse the use of) extraconstitutional means to change the government, such as military coups, violent insurrections, or mass protests aimed at forcing a change in the government?

- Do they attempt to undermine the legitimacy of elections, for example, by refusing to accept credible election results?

2. Denial of the legitimacy of political opponents

- Do they describe their rivals as subversive or opposed to the existing constitutional order?

- Do they claim that their rivals constitute an existential threat, either to national security or to the prevailing way of life?

- Do they baselessly describe their partisan rivals as criminals whose supposed violations of the law (or potential to do so) disqualify them from full participation in the political arena?

- Do they baselessly suggest that their rivals are foreign agents and that they are secretly working in alliance with (or in the employ of) a foreign government – usually an enemy one?

3. Toleration or encouragement of violence

- Do they have any ties to armed gangs, paramilitary forces, militias, guerrillas, or other organizations that engage in illicit violence?

- Have they or their partisan allies sponsored or encouraged mob attacks on opponents?

- Have they tacitly endorsed violence by their supporters by refusing to condemn it or punish it unambiguously?

- Have they praised (or refused to condemn) other significant acts of political violence, either in the past or elsewhere in the world?

4. Readiness to curtail the civil liberties of their opponents, including media

- Have they supported laws or policies that restrict civil liberties, such as expanded libel or defamation laws, or laws restricting protest, criticism of the government, or certain civic or political organizations?

- Have they threatened to take legal or other punitive actions against critics or rival parties, civil society, or the media?

- Have they praised repressive measures taken by other governments, either in the past or elsewhere in the world?

So, is our democracy so weak that it is vulnerable to the power of an authoritarian to weaken or even destroy our form of government? I believe the answer is yes. If our citizens are not diligent, this can happen before we know it. I will further assert that the seeds have been planted by our 45th President, Donald Trump. Keep in mind that I voted for him in 2016 but woke up in 2020 and voted for Joe Biden, who ran against him, even though I didn't agree with many of his policies.

Why do I believe this? What evidence is there?

Let's look at how our 45th President has measured up relative to the "Four Key Indicators of Authoritarian Behavior." First, he has, at the very least, a weak commitment to democratic rules. This is evidenced by his refusal to accept the election results of 2020. He attempted to have his Vice President, Mike Pence, violate his Constitutional duty and not certify the electoral votes that would validate Joe Biden as the winner. He is currently indicted in Georgia for leading a "criminal racketeering enterprise" to change the certified vote in Georgia. His 18 co-defendants are charged with following his lead and using several illegal means to accomplish this goal.

Second, Mr. Trump has shown no respect for his political opponents. Even though he desires to change our Constitution, he describes his rivals as subversive or opposed to the existing constitutional order. Ironically, he calls his rivals names that may just describe himself. Examples are "Crooked Hillary" and "Lyin' Ted." Other nicknames used to diminish his rivals (or those who oppose him) and excite his supporters are: "Low Energy Jeb," "Pocahontas," "Failing New York Times," "Crazy Maxine Waters," "Little Marco," and "Basement Biden." To make this worse, several news (maybe anti-news) networks regularly repeat these insulting names to satisfy Trump's supporters. Strangely, however, he never criticizes Vladimir Putin.

Third, the former President tolerates or encourages violence. During a debate leading up to the 2020 election, he demonstrated his support for a far-right militant organization by saying, "Proud Boys stand back and stand by." By doing so, he displayed his unwritten leadership of the group as well as his knowledge that they are there to follow him wherever he leads. He supported white supremacist groups when their riot in Charlottesville, Virginia, resulted in several injuries and a death.

His description of the rioters attempted to place them on the same level as the peaceful protesters who they attacked. He weakly stated that there were good people on both sides.

Furthermore, the most significant of these militant groups, such as the Proud Boys, the Oath Keepers, and the Three Percenters, along with Nazis and other white supremacist groups, marched onto and invaded the US Capitol on January 6, 2021. This happened after Trump led a pre-planned rally on the morning of the riot to incite the gangs to the Capitol. This resulted in several injuries and five deaths.

Fourth, he has attempted to curtail the civil liberties of his opponents by directly and/or through his followers seeking to deny certain citizens their legal right to cast their vote. An example is the fraudulent electoral ballot scheme that was implemented in seven states where Trump lost.

Trump has also consistently trashed any media entity that disagrees with his policies or bad conduct. This includes major newspapers, network news, along with cable networks such as MSNBC and CNN. If the media source won't endorse his lies and feed red meat to his followers, they are considered "enemies of the people."

As of September 2023, Donald Trump has currently been indicted for 91 felonies in four courts. Many of these charges relate to the actions described above. Oddly enough, however, he is the leading Republican candidate by a wide margin for the 2024 Presidential election. This should be a red flag for those who are concerned about the future of our democracy. If a former President who has been impeached twice (notwithstanding one of these being, I feel, politically motivated) and is facing 91 felonies can be seen by so many as qualified to be our next President, our democracy as we know it is in dire jeopardy.

Good citizens need to accept what is happening to our democracy, or they may wake up one day with the freedom that many Americans have fought and died for stripped away from them.

Crime and racism

Crime and racism have been with us since we formed our Union almost 250 years ago. Obviously, not everyone is a criminal or a racist. Those who are, however, are sabotaging the lives of many and, in some cases, severely impeding their ability to pursue their idea of happiness. These criminals and racists are missing my fundamental values of good citizens: LOVE and THE GOLDEN RULE.

The following are some takeaways from a report by the World Population Review:

The United States' crime rates rank in the middle of the pack worldwide, with overall crime decreasing over the past 25 years. The countries with the highest crime rates are Venezuela, Papua New Guinea, Afghanistan, Honduras, and Jamaica. The major causes of this for these countries are government corruption, gang activity, economic and social declines, poverty, assassinations, drug trade, etc.

Some of the lowest crime rates are in Switzerland, Denmark, Norway, Japan, and New Zealand. Each of these countries has very effective law enforcement, and Denmark, Norway, and Japan have some of the most restrictive gun laws in the world.

At the risk of repeating myself, the report indicated that the countries with the worst crime rates have unstable and corrupt governments, armed gang activity, poverty, and economic and social declines, while the countries with the lowest crime rates have effective law enforcement and restrictive gun laws.

The United States may be in the middle of the pack; however, serious crime problems do exist here at home. A significant one that is growing is school shootings. According to the *Washington Post*, more than 356,000 students have experienced gun violence since the Columbine school shooting in 1999.

Another growing concern is cybercrime. This type of crime has been a concern for businesses and individuals alike. This used to be a mild threat; however, as technology advances, threats to businesses and individuals are accelerating. Cybercrime accounts for over $1 trillion in losses annually, an amount that doubled in the past four years.

A byproduct of crime is racism. One example is antisemitism. CNN reported that antisemitic incidents in the U.S. reached their highest level since 1979. The incidents involving assault, vandalism, and harassment increased by more than a third in just one year and reached nearly 3,700 cases in 2022.

The most significant form of racism that still stains American society is that directed toward African Americans. This began in the colonial era when blacks were shipped from Europe to the American colonies for slave labor. At the time of the writing of our Declaration of Independence and Constitution, blacks were not considered free members of society. Even with the Civil War leading to the Emancipation Proclamation (essentially freeing the slaves), blacks were still seen as inferior by many citizens and continued to be the target of many hate crimes.

After the Emancipation Proclamation, the freedom of blacks was consistently impeded by politics and crime. Their social and economic freedom was constantly at risk and still is today. They have been subjected to lynchings, segregation, and Jim Crow laws. Furthermore, blacks' citizenship rights were constantly under attack. One significant example of this was their voting rights. In 1870, the 15th Amendment, for the first time, afforded blacks the right to vote. However, their participation was limited due to laws created, mainly by Southern legislatures, making it more and more difficult for them to participate. I believe it is still happening today, as shown by laws that have been enacted in Texas and Georgia to tighten control over who can easily exercise their voting rights.

As racism and crime swirl around our existence, none of us are truly free. America is approaching a crossroads. Do we learn and copy from countries like Venezuela or Honduras, or do we learn and copy from countries like Denmark, Norway, or Japan? The road we take during the remainder of the 21st century will be critical.

So, it begs the question: *Who are the criminals and racists? Why do they exist? Are our laws and statutes too weak to prevent such behavior? Can they be stopped?* The remaining decades of the 21st century will reveal many of the answers to these questions.

Remember, the solution may be simple but difficult to implement. It is never-ending LOVE and the ongoing application of THE GOLDEN RULE.

<u>Immigration</u>

Why does America, which is a country founded on immigration, face large immigration problems today?

North American ancestors of Native Americans have been inhabiting this area since as far back as the Ice Age. In the 17th century, to experience religious freedom and better economic opportunities, people from Great Britain, Spain, France, and Holland, as well as Pilgrims, arrived in the territory that eventually became the United States of America. As we discussed earlier, Africans were also imported for slave labor.

The History Channel outlined the following immigration timeline.

White People of 'Good Character' Granted Citizenship

January 1776: Thomas Paine published a pamphlet, "Common Sense," that argued for American independence. Most colonists considered themselves Britons, but Paine made the case for a new American. *"Europe, and not England, is the parent country of America. This new world hath been the asylum for the persecuted lovers of civil and religious liberty from every part of Europe,"* he writes.

March 1790: Congress passes the first law about who should be granted U.S. citizenship. The Naturalization Act of 1790 allows any free white person of "good character" who has been living in the United States for two years or longer to apply for citizenship. Without citizenship, nonwhite residents are denied basic constitutional protections, including the right to vote, own property, or testify in court.

August 1790: The first U.S. census takes place. The English are the largest ethnic group among the 3.9 million people counted, though nearly one in five Americans are of African heritage.

Irish Immigrant Wave

1815: Peace is re-established between the United States and Britain after the War of 1812. Immigration from Western Europe turned from a trickle into a gush, which caused a shift in the demographics of the United States. This first major wave of immigration lasted until the Civil War.

Between 1820 and 1860, the Irish—many of them Catholic—accounted for an estimated one-third of all immigrants to the United States. Some 5 million German immigrants also came to the United States, many of them making their way to the Midwest to buy farms or settle in cities including Milwaukee, St. Louis, and Cincinnati.

1819: Many newcomers arrive sick or dying from their long journey across the Atlantic in cramped conditions. The immigrants overwhelmed major port cities, including New York City, Boston, Philadelphia, and Charleston. In response, the United States passed the Steerage Act of 1819, requiring better conditions on ships arriving in the country. The Act also calls for ship captains to submit demographic information on passengers, creating the first federal records on the ethnic composition of immigrants to the United States.

1849: America's first anti-immigrant political party, the Know-Nothing Party, formed as a backlash to the increasing number of German and Irish immigrants settling in the United States.

1875: Following the Civil War, some states passed their own immigration laws. In 1875, the **Supreme Court** declared that it was the responsibility of the federal government to make and enforce immigration laws.

Chinese Exclusion Act

1880: As America began a rapid period of industrialization and urbanization, a second immigration boom began. Between 1880 and 1920, more than 20 million immigrants arrived. The majority were from Southern, Eastern and Central Europe, including 4 million Italians and 2 million Jews. Many of them settled in major U.S. cities and worked in factories.

1882: The **Chinese Exclusion Act** was passed, which barred Chinese immigrants from entering the United States. Beginning in the 1850s, a steady flow of Chinese workers had immigrated to America.

They worked in the gold mines and garment factories, built railroads, and took agricultural jobs. Anti-Chinese sentiment grew as Chinese laborers became successful in America. Although Chinese immigrants make up only 0.002 percent of the United States population, white workers blame them for low wages.

The 1882 Act was the first in American history to place broad restrictions on certain immigrant groups.

1891: The Immigration Act of 1891 further excluded who could enter the United States, barring the immigration of polygamists, people convicted of certain crimes, and the sick or diseased. The Act also created a federal office of immigration to coordinate immigration enforcement and a corps of immigration inspectors stationed at principal ports of entry.

Ellis Island Opens

January 1892: Ellis Island, the United States' first immigration station, opens in New York Harbor. The first immigrant processed was Annie Moore, a teenager from County Cork in Ireland. More than 12 million immigrants would enter the United States through Ellis Island between 1892 and 1954.

1907: U.S. immigration peaked, with 1.3 million people entering the country through Ellis Island alone.

February 1907: Amid prejudices in California that an influx of Japanese workers would cost white workers farming jobs and depress wages, the United States and Japan signed the Gentlemen's Agreement. Japan agreed to limit Japanese emigration to the United States to certain categories of business and professional men. In return, **President Theodore Roosevelt** urged San Francisco to end the segregation of Japanese students from white students in San Francisco schools.

1910: An estimated three-quarters of New York City's population consisted of new immigrants and first-generation Americans.

New Restrictions at the Start of WWI

1917: Xenophobia reaches new highs on the eve of American involvement in **World War I**. The **Immigration Act of 1917** established a literacy requirement for immigrants entering the country and halted immigration from most Asian countries.

May 1924: The Immigration Act of 1924 limited the number of immigrants allowed into the United States yearly through nationality quotas. Under the new quota system, the United States issued immigration visas to 2 percent of the total number of people of each nationality in the United States at the 1890 census. The law favors immigration from Northern and Western European countries. Just three countries, Great Britain, Ireland, and Germany, account for 70 percent of all available visas. Immigration from Southern, Central, and Eastern Europe was limited. The Act completely excluded immigrants from Asia, aside from the Philippines, which was an American colony at the time.

1924: In the wake of the numerical limit established by the 1924 law, illegal immigration to the United States increased. The U.S. Border Patrol was established to crack down on illegal immigrants crossing the Mexican and Canadian borders into the United States. Many of these early border crossers were Chinese and other Asian immigrants who had been barred from entering legally.

Mexicans Fill Labor Shortages During WWII

1942: Labor shortages during World War II prompted the United States and Mexico to form the Bracero Program, which allowed Mexican agricultural workers to enter the United States temporarily. The program lasted until 1964.

1948: The United States passed the nation's first refugee and resettlement law to deal with the influx of Europeans seeking permanent residence in the United States after World War II.

1952: The McCarran-Walter Act formally ended the exclusion of Asian immigrants from the United States.

1956-1957: The United States admitted roughly 38,000 immigrants from Hungary after a failed uprising against the Soviet Union. They were among the first Cold War refugees. The United States would admit over 3 million refugees during the Cold War.

1960-1962: Roughly 14,000 unaccompanied children flee Fidel Castro's Cuba and come to the United States as part of a secret, anti-Communism program called Operation Peter Pan.

Quota System Ends

1965: The Immigration and Nationality Act overhauled the American immigration system. The Act ended the national origin quotas enacted in the 1920s, which favored some racial and ethnic groups over others.

The quota system was replaced with a seven-category preference system emphasizing family reunification and skilled immigrants. Upon signing the new bill, President Lyndon B. Johnson called the old immigration system "un-American" and said the new bill would correct a "cruel and enduring wrong in the conduct of the American Nation."

Over the next five years, immigration from war-torn regions of Asia, including Vietnam and Cambodia, would more than quadruple. Family reunification became a driving force in U.S. immigration.

April-October 1980: During the Mariel boatlift, roughly 125,000 Cuban refugees made a dangerous sea crossing in overcrowded boats to arrive on the Florida shore seeking political asylum.

Amnesty to Undocumented Immigrants

1986: President Ronald Reagan signed into law the Simpson-Mazzoli Act, which grants amnesty to more than 3 million immigrants living illegally in the United States.

2001: U.S. Senators Dick Durbin (D-Ill.) and Orrin Hatch (R-Utah) propose the first Development, Relief, and Education of Alien Minors (DREAM) Act, which would provide a pathway to legal status for Dreamers, undocumented immigrants brought to the United States illegally by their parents as children. The bill—and subsequent iterations of it—didn't pass.

2012: President **Barack Obama** signed Deferred Action for Childhood Arrivals (DACA), which temporarily shields some Dreamers
from deportation but doesn't provide a path to citizenship.

2017: President **Donald Trump** issued two executive orders aimed at
curtailing travel and immigration from six majority-Muslim countries
(Chad, Iran, Libya, Syria, Yemen, Somalia) as well as North Korea
and Venezuela. Both so-called Muslim travel bans were challenged in
state and federal courts.

2018: In April 2018, the travel restrictions on Chad were lifted. In June
2018, the U.S. Supreme Court upheld a third version of the travel ban
on the remaining seven countries.

As we have ended our direct military involvement in Iraq and
Afghanistan, we have focused our attention more on immigration issues as they relate to America's Southern border. The four main issues
today are border security, humanitarian concerns, demographics, and
economic impact.

Some of the concerns related to these issues are (1) the handling
of refugees; (2) the citizenship rights of DREAMERS and the effect
of DACA (Deferred Action for Childhood Arrivals); (3) the disposi-
tion of those housed in Detention Centers; and (4) the cultural homog-
enization of Sanctuary Cities.

There are also elements of crime and racism that unfortunately
exist as part of the immigration concerns. Many Americans see immigrants, especially those from our Southern border, as taking jobs away
from qualified Americans. Some Americans also become xenophobic
(afraid of strangers), or they suffer from the "disease" of racism.

Immigration issues are not only America's problem but also a
problem in the countries from which the immigrants originate. Some
come from countries with poor potential for economic gains. Some
are refugees from war-torn and/or abusive and corrupt governments,
and some just want to be a part of America's dream for its citizens.

One key factor regarding immigration issues relating to our Southern border is the flood of migrants filtering into the US from Mexico. In my opinion, there are two "game-changing" solutions to this problem. (1) Mexican and American leaders must accept that it is a joint problem for both governments to work together and to create laws accordingly, and (2) expand this collaboration to include challenging the countries where the migrants are fleeing from to support their citizens more humanely. Without these two initiatives, the problem will only continue to grow.

<u>National Deficit and Debt</u>

The size and effect of Federal deficits and the National Debt have been a concern since they started growing in the 21st century. As recently as 2000, the United States had no budget deficit (actually a slight surplus) and a National Debt of $5.6 trillion, which was 55% of the GDP (Gross Domestic Product). Today, our National Debt is $32.9 trillion (122% of GDP), and the Federal deficit is approaching $2 trillion.

What has happened in the first 22-plus years of this century to cause this? The major contributors are: (1) the worldwide war on terrorism; (2) related wars in Afghanistan and Iraq; (3) recessions in 2001 and the Great Recession of 2008; (4) the pandemic of COVID-19; (5) rising interest rates in recent years to fight inflation; and (6) the aging population.

It should be noted that the effects of these issues have crossed the Presidential terms of both Democrats and Republicans. The breakdown of debt increases by President since 2000 are as follows:

- G. W. Bush – 2 terms - $3.05 trillion per term
- Obama – 2 terms - $4.1 trillion per term
- Trump – 1 term - $8.2 trillion
- Biden – 2/3 of a term - $4.5 trillion

US budget spending has grown from $1.46 trillion in 2000 to $6.4 trillion in 2023 (4.4 times). During the same period, GDP grew from $10.3 trillion to $27 trillion (2.6 times). Despite the political narrative to the contrary, this is a bi-partisan problem requiring bi-partisan solutions.

Why are ongoing (seemingly never-ending) budget deficits and the size of the National Debt so important?

The size of the National Debt *per se* is not considered a major problem today. However, suppose we continue to let it grow out of proportion to the growth of our GDP, encounter unexpected problems, and experience a significant rise in interest rates. In that case, major problems are around the corner. America, to remain competitive, cannot indefinitely continue to borrow more than it produces.

The world is looking at us. They see our vulnerability, which is evident with our leaders continually fighting over things like debt limits, temporary spending bills, finger-pointing regarding government shutdowns, etc. Because of politics, our leaders cannot even work together on a productive annual budget process. They argue in ways that are misleading to the public. They think we are stupid. Their goals are to get re-elected and control us.

One of the biggest contributors to our growing National Debt is mandatory spending. The citizens of the United States believe that their key entitlements—Social Security, Medicare, and Medicaid—are protected by a trust fund. This is not true. The payroll taxes that are received to fund these entitlements are grouped with other revenue to be available to pay all US obligations (mandatory or discretionary). What is an even bigger problem is that these payroll taxes do not fund Medicaid and are dependent on other government revenue.

Let's look at what constitutes the elements of the US budget.

Discretionary Spending (in trillions)

Revenue	*$2,901*
Discretionary Expenses	*$1,753*
Interest on Debt	*$652*
Net Discretionary Surplus	*$496*

Deficit for Social Security & Medicare (in trillions)

Revenue	*$1,567*
Expenses	*$2,149*
*Net Deficit **for Social Security &** Medicare*	*$582*

Deficits for Medicaid & Other Unfunded Mandatory (in trillions)

Revenue	*0*
Medicaid	*$594*
Other Unfunded Mandatory	*$1,248*
Net Deficit for Medicaid & Other Unfunded Mandatory	*$1,842*

Total US Budget

Revenue	*$4,468*
Expenses	*$6,396*
Deficit	*$1,928*

These statistics are a combination of CBO estimates and actual revenue and expenses through early September 2023. I believe that they are very close projections to where the budget activity will close out by the end of the fiscal year, September 30, 2023.

These statistics point out one significant issue. $1.842 trillion of the total US deficit of $1.928 trillion (or 95.5%) is caused by Medicaid and Other Unfunded Mandatory Expenses. The US has a surplus in Discretionary Expenses. The other issue of concern is the deficit in Social Security and Medicare spending. The deficit related to Social Security and Medicare is growing toward insolvency faster than hoped.

Our government leaders need to honor the trust that was provided to them by the American citizens who elected them to reconcile these concerns diligently and collaboratively. Their actions today are counterproductive. We must do better.

I have an idea. How about Democrats and Republicans collaborating to face the issues head-on and agree on the compromise required to solve whatever is solvable at this time? Then, just maybe, we can begin a process that will demonstrate that they can lead in a manner that we elected them to do.

The grip that Media holds on our lives!

Citizens need to wake up. We are allowing the media to control our thinking and actions without a complete understanding of where, how, and why the major media sources are disseminating information to us. Is the information from media sources based on the truth? Do they have a political agenda? Is their mission based on education for the public or controlling how we think? Is their profit motive more important to them than their responsibility to deliver fair and useful news?

In a rapidly changing world, it is more important than ever to receive fair and accurate information on issues close to home and around the world. This is impossible today with the amount of media bias that our major news outlets are demonstrating. A 2015 article by Alexander Peters entitled "The Issues in Media Today" described this problem very well.

"Major news organizations such as Fox News and MSNBC are some of the most well-known news organizations in the United States and relay most of the news to the everyday citizen who cares enough to watch their broadcasts. This would be perfectly fine if these two networks were not notoriously known for going out of their way to pander to conservative and liberal audiences, respectively, all for the sake of keeping their ratings as high as they possibly can. They will get the news across to the masses in a way that feeds them the bias that they decide fits them the best. This is a problem as many Americans only have the time and/or patience to watch the news on one channel. This means that they are not only presented with the story in a biased way but also do not even get to hear both sides of a story before they form an opinion about the topics."

Mr. Peters went on to write…

"Aside from swaying the public to have a certain bias because of what news network they watch, this can also obstruct the facts in a way that supports their bias. Fox News is probably the best known for messing up stories due to the powerful conservative bias they put on their newscasts, but MSNBC is guilty of factual inaccuracies, as well, due to liberal bias. This can cause news watchers to retain inaccurate information from these newscasts in a way that makes them look ignorant and uneducated in conversations on news topics with their peers."

"These inaccuracies are not only used by the big news television organizations, but also smaller news websites. In readings from the Conservative Tribune, it is apparent that the bias that they put forth is used to show a strong conservative view, which, in many cases, can cause the actual problems that a particular news story brings to light to be overshadowed due to the twist that the writers put on the story. I am not saying that this is due to the conservative views of the author, but in fact, the bias in the writings. Biases in the news can turn the focal point of a story from racial hate to discrimination against Christians or vice versa. And with these extremely biased websites being well read on social media outlets such as Facebook, it causes the news to be skewed information while being relayed to the general public."

The type of media described by Mr. Peters has continued to grow in the eight years following the publishing of the article. Biased media is controlling our thinking and actions and is breaking apart our society.

These eight years have seen two Presidential elections. The 2020 election was baselessly declared as fraudulent by the Republican loser. The US court system at all levels supported the fact that it was a fair election. Notwithstanding court rulings, the lies related to the election results were peddled by the Republican loser to his right-wing supporters. All these actions led to a rally in Congress where an insurrection occurred in an attempt to violate Constitutional protocol.

The media lied, the supporters relied, and people died. As a result, our democracy is on the verge of a divide.

The result of the unreliability of the media today is that it is resulting in unabashed tribalism. We discussed the pitfalls of tribalism in Chapter 5 and described it as one of the major roadblocks to becoming a good citizen.

If the media continues on its current path, the people will not know what is really happening. The resultant ignorance will put our democracy on a slippery slope.

Climate change and global warming

Yes, Alice, climate change is happening and is one of the key issues facing the world in the 21st century. Of course, climate change has been happening since the beginning of time. However, it is accelerating faster today than ever before. Extensive scientific research has validated this.

Melting glaciers and more intense heat waves are occurring. Also, the effect of human-made greenhouse gases will continue to create severe weather damage that will only intensify over time.

NASA defines climate change as follows:

"Climate change is a long-term change in the average weather patterns that have come to define Earth's local, regional, and global climates. These changes have a broad range of observed effects that are synonymous with the term.

Changes observed in Earth's climate since the mid-20th century are driven by human activities, particularly fossil fuel burning, which increases heat-trapping greenhouse gas levels in Earth's atmosphere, raising Earth's average surface temperature. Natural processes, which have been overwhelmed by human activities, can also contribute to climate change, including internal variability (e.g., cyclical ocean patterns like El Niño, La Niña, and the Pacific Decadal Oscillation) and external forcings (e.g., volcanic activity, changes in the Sun's energy output, variations in Earth's orbit).

Scientists use observations from the ground, air, and space, along with computer models, to monitor and study past, present, and future climate change. Climate data records provide evidence of climate change key indicators, such as global land and ocean temperature increases; rising sea lev-

els; ice loss at Earth's poles and in mountain glaciers; frequency and severity changes in extreme weather such as hurricanes, heatwaves, wildfires, droughts, floods, and precipitation; and cloud and vegetation cover changes."

NASA's distinction between climate change and global warming:

"Climate change" and "global warming" are often used interchangeably but have distinct meanings.

Global warming is the long-term heating of the Earth's surface observed since the pre-industrial period (between 1850 and 1900) due to human activities, primarily fossil fuel burning, which increases heat-trapping greenhouse gas levels in Earth's atmosphere. This term is not interchangeable with the term "climate change."

Since the pre-industrial period, human activities are estimated to have increased Earth's global average temperature by about 1 degree Celsius (1.8 degrees Fahrenheit), a number that is currently increasing by more than 0.2 degrees Celsius (0.36 degrees Fahrenheit) per decade. The current warming trend is unequivocally the result of human activity since the 1950s and has proceeded at an unprecedented rate over millennia.

Climate change and global warming are resulting in extreme conditions worldwide. These have caused increases in natural disasters such as droughts, wildfires, tropical cyclones, floods, heat waves, etc. These can only intensify as the world population continues to increase.

As described, climate change and global warming are creating an apocalyptic situation. This doesn't have to be the case. First of all, we need to accept that there is a problem. Listen to the experts and not be distracted by media bias. If good citizens don't allow themselves to be ignorant of the issues and diligently seek solutions, climate change, and global warming can be curtailed by the end of the 21st century.

<u>Health issues</u>

After a century of life expectancy increases in the 20th century, the 21st century is starting to introduce Americans to a reversal in that trend. In 1900, life expectancy was 47 years. By 1950, it had grown to 68 years, and by 2019, it had risen to 79 years. However, in 2020, it fell to 77, and in 2021, it fell to 76. According to a report from the Harvard Medical School, the major contributors to this trend are COVID-19, drug overdoses, and accidental injuries. Other contributors included heart disease, liver disease, and suicides.

We have already addressed that poverty and food insecurity are major concerns that are being experienced around the world today, including in the United States. A lack of access to healthcare adds to these problems, resulting in a reduced life expectancy.

The Harvard report also presents other health measures such as infant mortality, maternal mortality, vaccination rates, and cancer screening rates.

It should be noted that even though the life expectancy statistic is lower in 2021, more Americans than ever are reaching the age of 100 (almost 90,000) at this time. Medical advances, along with lifestyle changes and a rapid growth in population, have contributed to this. Other factors are gender and parental age.

Notwithstanding pandemics, drug and alcohol addiction, suicides, and natural disasters, the major 21st-century healthcare concerns are chronic diseases, heart disease, Alzheimer's, and obesity. This is an area where good citizens have an opportunity to make a difference since such conditions are controllable through medical advances and personal lifestyle changes. These are also the major drivers of increasing healthcare costs at this time.

The Institute for Health Metrics and Evaluation (IHME) lists 11 global health issues to watch in 2023 and beyond. They are:

- Long COVID
- Mental health
- Climate change
- Cardiovascular disease
- Lower respiratory infections
- Poverty's role in health
- Need for strengthening health systems
- Diabetes
- Road injuries
- Dementia
- Population aging

Artificial Intelligence

The Artificial Intelligence (AI) landscape covers more territory than most people can imagine. This includes everything from chatbots to machine learning and even virtual companions and cyber security, to mention only a few.

When people talk about AI, they typically envision robots controlling our lives. An Oxford dictionary definition of AI is: "the study and development of computer systems that can copy intelligent human behaviour."

An article by Nisha Arya Ahmed in the *AI Time Journal* in February 2023 helps us get a better understanding of AI and how it affects us today.

In the world of technology and computer science, Artificial Intelligence relates to human-like intelligence constructed by a computer. It refers to the capability of a computer/machine to imitate the characteristics of the human brain by replicating its intelligence.

A Brief History of AI

Let's look into the history of AI. In the mid-1950s, John McCarthy was known as the father of artificial intelligence for creating the term AI. For him, his definition of AI is "the science and engineering of making intelligent machines." Some may know him for creating Lisp, which is a programming language used in robotics for different types of Internet services. He started working on self-driving cars to create programs that understand the human brain better and imitate the way humans make decisions. Many of us use Cloud computing services, where we can share data between people. This was another of McCarthy's innovations.

The surge in the development of artificial intelligence is primarily dependent on the access of large amounts of data and the evolution of technology, allowing the data process and manipulation to be better than humans. Artificial Intelligence can do everything we humans can do, from giving us directions to medical analysis.

Some further examples of AI today are Amazon's Alexa and Apple Siri, which help us create potential links on what we may want to purchase based on our current searches, being able to recognize spam emails whilst also helping us detect fraud.

There are two broad types of Artificial Intelligence:

1. Narrow AI

2. General AI

Narrow AI

Narrow AI is the type of AI that performs a single take. It's being able to carry out specific tasks that intelligent systems have been taught without being sophistically programmed, and this is why it's called Narrow AI. To give you a better understanding, it's Siri for Apple users. Examples of this are self-driving cars and voice recognition to help radiologists pick up tumors.

Machine and Deep Learning

Narrow AI is based on machine learning and deep learning. A better way to understand what you just read: AI is constructed on a set of algorithms that try to imitate human intelligence. Machine learning is one of these algorithms, and deep learning is a sub-skill of a machine learning technique.

Machine learning consumes data and uses statistics to better learn the data, in turn improving the ability to solve the task.

Machine learning is made up of both supervised and unsupervised learning. Supervised learning learns on a labeled dataset, allowing you to produce outputs based on previous data. In contrast, Unsupervised learning uses unlabeled data to learn about and discover unknown patterns in data.

Deep learning, also known as deep neural learning, is a type of machine learning technique that tries to imitate the human brain by inputting data through a biological-inspired neural network that contains a number of hidden layers. Through the hidden layers, the data is processed, making connections and creating patterns.

General AI

General AI has a bit more complexity to it and tries to mirror human intellect using its ability to learn and apply the knowledge learned to solve problems. We are now going through the process of transitioning from Narrow AI to General AI, for example, natural language processing. In order to achieve this, computer hardware needs to advance in computational power to perform at a better rate.

Examples of AI Applications

Below are some examples of AI applications to give you a better understanding of how it has been implemented:

- *Speech recognition: This is the process of enabling a computer to recognize spoken words and have the ability to respond, for example, Siri.*

- *Natural Language Processing: This enables software to understand, interpret, and generate the human language, for example, language translation and email filtering.*

- *Image recognition: This process can classify text, people, and objects as well as moving images. Examples of this are fingerprint ID systems, self-driving cars, and face recognition.*

__These are only a few examples of where AI has evolved, and we hope this has helped you on your early journey in the world of Artificial Intelligence and the evolution of technology.__

Ahmed's article helps us understand how AI has grown in the past 70+ years. As AI-capable machines absorb technology advances and more data, the possibilities are endless. This AI growth will expand and continue throughout the 21st century and beyond.

In earlier parts of this book, we have shown the human traits of citizens in several different ways. We have mentioned the importance of learning, problem-solving, reasoning, creativity, and social behavior. As we do this, we gather knowledge. Computers can also think and act based on increased data, just as humans do.

Humans have sensory and cognitive components that machines can replicate. Today, uses such as driving a car or playing chess are based on narrow AI. However, the long-term goal of many researchers is to create General AI where humans can be outperformed in every single task.

AI's capacity to change our lives is limitless. Until now, advances in AI have led to positive advances in the lives of humans. Will all future drivers of AI keep us on that track, or will some seek to sabotage our existence?

For instance, many experts are concerned that AI could lead to a nuclear-level catastrophe. This concern centers around the thought that AI is growing too fast. Also, as AI learns to improve itself, we don't know how to control it; and further, the speed at which AI learns can be thousands of times faster than humans.

Mike Thomas wrote an article that was updated by Brennan Whitfield in August 2023 that listed 12 risks and dangers of AI. They are:

1. Lack of AI Transparency and Explainability
2. Job Losses Due to Automation

3. Social Manipulation through AI Algorithms
4. Social Surveillance with AI Technology
5. Lack of Data Privacy Using AI Tools
6. Biases due to AI
7. Socioeconomic Inequality as a result of AI
8. Weakening Ethics and Goodwill because of AI
9. Autonomous Weapons Powered by AI
10. Financial Crisis brought about by AI Algorithms
11. Loss of Human Influence
12. Uncontrollable Self-aware AI

AI is a big deal. How humans control its growth and usage is a major 21st-century issue.

<u>Nuclear War Concerns</u>

The creation and use of nuclear weapons was a 20th-century project begun in the 1930s by the United Kingdom. During World War II, the UK partnered with the United States with input from Canada on "The Manhattan Project," creating a weapon using nuclear fission. This resulted in the only use of nuclear weapons in armed conflict by the United States against Japan in 1945. Shortly after this, Britain, France, and the Soviet Union began developing their nuclear weapons. It should be noted that, after the breakup of the Soviet Union in 1991, four of the former Soviet republics now also have nuclear weapons (Belarus, Kazakhstan, Ukraine, and, of course, Russia).

Other countries known to have nuclear war capabilities are Israel, India, Pakistan, China, and North Korea. In addition, it appears that Iran also has nuclear war capacity; however, they have alleged that they only have them for peaceful use.

One thought-provoking statistic is that 90% of the world's nuclear warheads exist in Russia and the United States.

Currently, any country with the know-how can make nuclear weapons. However, not all are allowed to do so due to the creation of the Treaty on the Non-Proliferation of Nuclear Weapons (NPT). The purpose of the NPT was to prevent the spread of nuclear weapons and to promote disarmament.

According to a report by BBC News, since 1970, 191 states, including the US, Russia, the UK, France, and China, have joined the NPT. These five countries are called nuclear-weapon states – and are allowed to have weapons because they built and tested a nuclear explosive device before the treaty came into effect on 1 January 1967.

The BBC report further states that, even though these countries have nuclear weapons, under the agreement, they have to reduce how many they have and can't keep them forever.

It was further noted that Israel (which has never confirmed or denied the existence of its nukes), India, and Pakistan have never joined the NPT, and North Korea left in 2003.

Iran, who has agreed to elements of the NPT, pulled out of it after 2018.

What does all of this mean? Are there still nuclear war concerns? I believe the answer is yes. As long as nuclear weapons exist at all, the world remains threatened by the potential of nuclear war. The extent of the world's nuclear weapons has been reduced from 140,000 in 1986 to approximately 70,000 today. Interestingly enough, while the US and Russia have been reducing their stockpiles, China, India, Pakistan, and North Korea have been increasing theirs, according to the Federation of American Scientists.

Even though there may be fewer nukes today, the world remains vulnerable.

A major question that needs to be asked is: "Are nuclear weapons a war deterrent or a catalyst for war?" I pray that they serve as a war deterrent and promote peace. However, we need to accept the risk that nuclear arms may be a weapon of war.

Global Tensions

In the previous section, we explored a global concern that has the capacity to change the world as we know it by destroying segments of its existence. In addition, and partially along with nuclear war concerns, there are examples of other global tensions that exist in the world today. They are Russia's invasion of Ukraine; pressure by China toward Taiwan and other countries in the region; cyber-attacks aimed mainly at the infrastructure of the US; North Korea's testing of nuclear weapons and its impact on the region; military confrontations between Israel and Iran; the expanding migration of people from Central America and Mexico, mainly due to violence, corruption, political unrest, and poor economic conditions in their native countries.

Actually, I see these as the major concerns of the United States. However, many other nations around the world are experiencing major issues affecting their freedom and peaceful way of life. These span all of the seven continents of the globe.

Early in 2023, the US was keeping abreast of all material conflicts in the world that may affect its interests. For the last 15 years, the Council on Foreign Relations Center for Preventive Action (CPA), with support from Carnegie Corporation of New York, has been asking foreign policy experts to evaluate 30 ongoing or potential conflicts based on their likelihood of occurring in the coming year and their impact on U.S. interests.

In addition to war-related concerns, these global tensions are currently and/or have the capacity to change our lives in many ways in the future. Many of these relate to other 21st-century issues that we have previously mentioned. They are food security, increased crime, economic challenges, climate control, health concerns, and even attacks on our democracy.

The Global Risk Report of 2023 by the World Economic Forum describes major issues that they see being a concern for the next ten years. The Report states as follows:

For the past 17 years, the World Economic Forum's Global Risks Report has warned about deeply interconnected global risks. Conflict and geo-economic tensions have triggered a series of deeply interconnected global risks, according to the World Economic Forum's Global Risks Report 2023. These include energy and food supply crunches, which are likely to persist for the next two years, and strong increases in the cost of living and debt servicing. At the same time, these crises risk undermining efforts to tackle longer-term risks, notably those related to climate change, biodiversity, and investment in human capital.

These are the findings of the Global Risks Report 2023, released today, which argues that the window for action on the most serious long-term threats is closing rapidly, and concerted, collective action is needed before risks reach a tipping point.

The report, produced in partnership with Marsh McLennan and Zurich Insurance Group, draws on the views of over 1,200 global risk experts, policymakers, and industry leaders. Across three timeframes, it paints a picture of the global risks landscape that is both new and eerily familiar, as the world faces many pre-existing risks that previously appeared to be receding.

At present, the global pandemic and war in Europe have brought energy, inflation, food, and security crises back to the fore. These create follow-on risks that will dominate the next two years: the risk of recession, growing debt distress, a continued cost of living crisis, polarized societies enabled by disinformation and misinformation, a hiatus on rapid climate action, and zero-sum geo-economic warfare.

Unless the world starts to cooperate more effectively on climate mitigation and climate adaptation over the next 10 years, this will lead to continued global warming and ecological breakdown. Failure to mitigate and adapt to climate change, natural disasters, biodiversity loss, and environmental degradation represent five of the top 10 risks – with biodiversity loss seen as one of the most rapidly deteriorating global risks over the next decade. In parallel, crises-driven leadership and geopolitical rivalries risk creating societal distress at an unprecedented level as investments in health, education, and economic development disappear, further eroding social cohesion. Finally, rising rivalries risk not only growing geo-economic weaponization but also remilitarization, especially through new technologies and rogue actors.

In summary, there is much tension in the world. Many countries conflict with one another. There is also growing infighting within many countries, especially the United States. Unless our leaders find some way to collaborate respectfully to solve the problems for which they have been elected, there is little or no hope of solving the major problems of the day. They have forgotten, or worse, never cared about the importance of LOVE and THE GOLDEN RULE.

Education

In the last chapter, I referenced the absence of knowledge or ignorance as one of the six key roadblocks to people becoming good citizens. Additionally, in Chapter 2, I cited education and lifetime learning as major responsibilities of every good citizen. In this chapter, I would like to go further and show how educated citizens are essential to solving 21st-century issues.

A report by the Harvard Advanced Leadership Initiative entitled "Education for the 21st Century" addresses the concerns regarding education as we move forward in this century. The report discusses ways that the skills that students develop in schools must align with economic revitalization and growth, civic participation, and democratic engagement. The report went further to discuss ways for schools to balance the goals of fostering academic excellence with doing this fairly for all students.

The following is quoted from the report's Executive Summary and explains the issues very clearly. The consensus of the panel who wrote the report was that....

"The educational system in the United States needs serious attention. Student achievement results are mediocre in international comparisons; too many students drop out of school before completing high school, many students begin community college or college poorly prepared to meet the academic requirements, college completion is low, and many of those who do graduate are not seen by employers as ready for the workforce. In addition, there are significant inequalities in that students from socially disadvantaged backgrounds, as well as African American and Latino students, are more likely to receive low-quality instruction, less likely to graduate from high school, or transition to college. These results stem from a disconnected system among different education levels, between education institutions and communities, and between education and social institutions. These poor education results undermine U.S. competitiveness, reproduce and increase social inequality, and overall diminish the capacities of people to have good healthy incomes to engage with their communities.

This worsening situation demands urgent improvement in education.

Alongside current problems, employers civil and social leaders increasingly see that the educational system needs to develop a new set of 21st century skills for students. Without new efforts to help students gain the competencies that prepare them to meet the demands of democracy, competitiveness, and life, schools are increasingly irrelevant. These competencies include critical thinking, collaboration, communication skills, and creativity. Other important skills include life skills, capacity for lifelong learning, technological and financial literacy, global awareness, and skills for effective civic engagement. These 21st-century skills are not limited to the United States; other countries are also reforming their education system in ways that align with these broader purposes, and some, such as Singapore, appear to be making more progress in aligning curriculum, teacher education, assessment systems, and other supports in ways that help educators teach to these 21st-century skills.

The development of these 21st-century skills is a necessary but challenging endeavor. The educational system has multiple stakeholders and is slow and difficult to change. Changes must be transformational and systemic rather than incremental, including the alteration of the entire educational paradigm through collaboration and community focus. New types of schools, leaders, instructional processes, and teachers are necessary to accomplish this effort.

Numerous programs and initiatives are producing outstanding results, revealing positive advancement. Schools are transformed, students are engaged, and remarkable results are achieved. The foremost challenge is scaling these successes and devising a system to learn from these positive deviations, educators, and institutions that are succeeding against the odds.

Education transformation does not necessarily require new ideas, programs, or interventions but rather an identification of education that works domestically and internationally, then creating networks and collaborations to scale successful models. The field of education needs Advanced Leaders to form and lead collaborative, cross-sector, multi-stakeholder coalitions that bring multiple individuals and groups together, working toward a common vision. Advanced Leaders can further innovate and scale successful models and, in doing so, will improve the lives of children and the competitiveness and future of America."

There are examples today of corporate America working with school systems to prepare some of the students for jobs in their organizations. This not only teaches the students skills but also prepares them for a job and maybe even a career. Most of these corporate/school partnerships also teach the students soft skills related to their general conduct and how to work as part of a team.

In her book, *Good Power*, Ginni Rometty, former Chairman and CEO of IBM, outlined a successful program she founded called "P-TECH" that answered a question that bothered her, "Why was there such a mismatch between the demand for tech talent and the supply?"

Ms. Rometty worked with a school in Brooklyn, New York, to create a program that would accomplish a few important goals required to turn the participating students into productive workers. IBM designed a six-year program and assisted in the funding. The program operated in the Brooklyn school and acted as a dual enrollment in high school and community college. This provided the student with an opportunity for a debt-free education and a good job upon graduation. Initially, it worked to create learning skills in programming and mobile app development.

Candidates were those interested in STEM (science, technology, engineering, and math) fields. Those who completed the P-TECH certificate were dedicated, partially because their classroom work was combined with paid internships.

Another interesting part of the program was that P-TECH first taught students critical skills like problem-solving and how to work in teams. Hard skills like programming were the least of the problems; many of those could be taught later by employers.

Eventually, other corporations participated in the P-TECH program by mentoring and helping the high school, and community colleges identify skills and curriculum students needed to learn to be employable. P-TECH was growing, with these participating students starting to fill needed jobs at IBM.

Ginni didn't stop there. She noticed the need to provide black and underserved communities with a similar opportunity to have careers in 21st-century technology companies. With this in mind, she collaborated with Ken Frazier, CEO of Merck, to launch a start-up called "OneTen." OneTen initially focused on black students and eventually included other underserved groups.

As this program grew, more than 60 major corporations participated, such as ADP, Allstate, American Express, AT&T, Bank of America, Cisco, Delta, GM, to name a few. According to Ginni, as more businesses signed up, each identified anywhere from 50 to 500 positions that qualified as a potential OneTen job to fill, which meant it paid a family-sustaining living wage, didn't require a four-year degree or more than five years of experience, and was not at risk of being automated out of existence.

I know I got a little bit more into the solutions that I planned. However, after reading Ginni's book, I couldn't let go of *Good Power* and just had to use her successful example here.

I would like to close this chapter with a quote from Ginni.

CHAPTER SEVEN

Addressing 21st-Century Issues

"If I had an hour to solve a problem, I'd spend 55 minutes thinking about the problem and 5 minutes thinking about the solutions."

- Albert Einstein

"No problem can stand the assault of sustained thinking."
- Voltaire

"How you think about a problem is more important than the problem itself. So always think positively."
- Norman Vincent Peale

"Intellectuals solve problems. Geniuses prevent them."

- Albert Einstein

In Chapter 1, I referred to 13 documents and speeches that appeared at critical times during our country's development. They were taken from Richard Brookhiser's book, *Give Me Liberty*. The ideas generated by these documents and speeches laid the foundation from which our society was given the opportunity to be a free country for all of its people.

Let's now revisit how these documents and speeches did this. I will now add the approximate dates they emerged.

1. Minutes of the Jamestown General Assembly (1619) defined the rules by which we self-govern.

2. The Flushing Remonstrance (1657) laid the foundation for freedom of religion.

3. The Trial of John Peter Zenger (1735) provided us with freedom of speech.

4. The Declaration of Independence (1776) cited that our Creator gave us certain inalienable rights, among those being life, liberty, and the pursuit of happiness.

5. The Manumission Society Constitution (1785) made significant strides in liberating enslaved people.

6. The Constitution of the United States (1789) defines how our federal government is to operate, distinguishes between Federal and State powers, and protects various individual liberties of free citizens.

7. The Monroe Doctrine (1823) further explained that the Western Hemisphere represents freedom from individual leaders, and there should be no kings here.

8. The Seneca Falls Declaration (1848) called for voting rights for women.

9. The Gettysburg Address (1863) provided a eulogy to our fallen soldiers and stated that "we are better than this" while embracing the Declaration of Independence and the Constitution.

10. The New Colossus (1883) welcomed the world to take part in our liberty. However, the Statue of Liberty did challenge those who would like to participate. As Brookhiser paraphrases, "Come here, be like us, I will show you the way. "

11. The Cross of Gold Speech (1896) further defined us as a nation with economic equality.

12. The Arsenal of Democracy Fireside Chat (1940) made an impression on the free world that Nazism is evil and Britain should be free of it.

13. The Tear Down That Wall (1987) speech sought to eliminate Communists as a ruling class in Europe.

All of these examples of patriotism had the same common denominator. That is, citizens with a purpose to make the United States (by example) and the world at large, a better place for all. They all had *love* and *the golden rule* in their hearts. Without these brave citizens, we may have never had an America, and if we did, we may have lost it in the 19th and 20th centuries.

In Chapter 6, I outlined 12 issues that confront mankind and have the capacity to wreck our freedom, shorten our lives, end our democracy, and even destroy our existence. I captured them with the acronym **FACING CHANGE**. In order to address these issues in the remainder of the 21st century, a new mindset must be developed. I call this the **CHANGING FACE**. The components of CHANGING FACE are as follows:

Collaboration

Humanism

Adaptability

Nobleness

Generosity

Innovation

Natural Learning

Grounded in Values

Failing Forward

Ambition

Creativity

Expediency

These are the characteristics that I see as vitally important for citizens to take the next step toward solving the problems that will face us for the rest of this century. Do you see these qualities in the leaders who were responsible for the 13 documents and speeches I cited? Of course, you do.

Taken as a whole, CHANGING FACE means to me that new paradigms may need to be created to solve substantial problems. This will require *a commitment to understand history in order to understand the issues better* before we tackle potential solutions. It is crucial, also, to make every attempt possible, not only to solve the problem but to devise a solution to prevent it from happening again. Let me provide an excellent example of this… Social Security.

The History Channel took a deep dive into the challenges of Social Security. Excerpts follow:

> *The Social Security Act was signed into law by Franklin D. Roosevelt in 1935. It created Social Security as a federal safety net for the elderly, unemployed, and disadvantaged Americans. The main stipulation of the original Social Security Act was to pay financial benefits to retirees over age 65 based on lifetime payroll tax contributions.*
>
> *Until Franklin D. Roosevelt became president, most social assistance plans in America were dependent on the government, charities, and private citizens doling out money to people in need.*
>
> *Roosevelt, however, borrowed a page from Europe's economic security rulebook and took a different approach. He proposed a program*

in which people contributed to their own future economic security by contributing a portion of their work income through payroll tax deductions.

Basically, the current working generation would pay into the program and finance the retired generation's monthly allowance.

In June 1934, President Roosevelt created the Committee on Economic Security (CES) and tasked them with creating an economic security bill. Led by the first woman to hold a U.S. cabinet post, Secretary of Labor Frances Perkins, the CES drafted the Social Security Act aimed at giving people economic security throughout their lives.

After much debate, Congress passed the Social Security Act to provide benefits to retirees based on their earnings history, and on August 14, 1935, Roosevelt signed it into law. This firmly placed the burden of economic security for American citizens on the federal government's shoulders.

Many amendments have been passed to the original Social Security Act. For instance, originally, monthly payouts of old-age benefits were slated to start on January 1, 1942. Eligible people who turned 65 prior to that date received a lump sum payment.

On August 10, 1939, an amendment passed to move up the start date to receive monthly benefits to January 1, 1940. Another amendment extended eligibility to dependents and survivors of retired workers.

In the 1950s, amendments were made which extended Social Security eligibility to domestic and farm workers, non-farm self-employed professionals, and some federal employees. It also offered voluntary coverage to some state and federal employees, hundreds of thousands of non-profit employees, and workers in the Virgin Islands and Puerto Rico.

By 1977, it was clear Social Security was in financial peril. An amendment was passed, changing the benefit qualification formula for people born after 1917. Other amendments were also passed, including increasing the payroll tax and slightly decreasing benefits to help cut costs, leaving some beneficiaries with less money during difficult economic times.

These efforts didn't prevent the program from facing a serious financial crisis in the 1980s, however, and President Ronald Reagan created a commission to examine how to keep Social Security in the black. In 1983, he signed legislation that gradually increased the retirement age to 67, taxed Social Security benefits, and provided Social Security benefits to federal workers.

After taking office in 2001, President George W. Bush appointed another Social Security Commission with its top priority being Social Security reform. No revolutionary changes were made to keep the program solvent long-term.

President Obama's administration temporarily reduced the Social Security tax rate from 6.2 to 4.2 percent in 2011 and 2012. The move helped ease the financial strain on American workers but did little to stop the risk of Social Security going into future debt.

The Social Security Act has provided Americans with much-needed financial help when they need it most. For many of America's most vulnerable, it's the only source of income they have.

Still, despite attempts to keep it solvent, the Social Security program faces a major long-term shortfall. The retirement age to receive full benefits continues to increase, and many beneficiaries are claiming benefits much later in life to receive maximum payouts, often at age 70.

As partisan politicians continue to debate the problem each year, the Social Security Administration—which is now an independent government agency—works behind the scenes to keep Social Security intact. Administering the program is a monumental and always-changing task.

Each year, the Social Security Administration rolls out changes to the program. In 2018, they announced a two percent cost-of-living adjustment, a taxable earnings increase, an earnings limit increase

I think that a very high percentage of Americans believe in the merits of Social Security. However, it is an example of a good plan that has gone awry. Several presidential administrations have made changes to the Social Security rules in an attempt to keep them solvent. Some actually worked against its solvency.

Our leaders in Washington are now faced with a dilemma: Do they use appropriate actuarial tools to make the necessary changes and inform the public that certain members of society will be negatively affected by them? Or do they ignore the issue and hope the voters are too ignorant to know that the Social Security "fund" will be insolvent in just a few years? The first choice will result in temporary pain for some but result in long-term solvency for the plan. The second will dodge the issue and keep the electorate focused on other issues that will seek to get leaders re-elected and put the system at risk for all.

Social Security is an example of why we not only need to fully understand a problem but also make sure our solution will stand the test of time and act quickly to amend the plan when new circumstances arise. Misguided politics is preventing our leaders from following these steps.

Now, let's see how the components of CHANGING FACE act to enhance challenging problem-solving and are critical for good citizens to address 21st century issues properly.

Please note that I will be addressing the *tools* necessary for good citizens to solve the problems of the 21st century instead of comprehensive solutions to the problems. I am doing this for two reasons: (1)

proper solutions to these problems are so complex that they require another book; (2) I believe that the *tools used to solve the problems* are more important. Without these characteristics, citizens will be too helpless to tackle these critical issues.

COLLABORATION

All of the participants in "Brookhiser's 13" used collaborative tools to address the changes they wanted to occur. Many of the issues they faced affected their livelihood and, in some cases, survival. To solve these problems, they needed support from their fellow man, including new ideas to solve the problems they faced. Therefore, they were forced to collaborate with others who faced the same issues in order to build a consensus and strengthen their cause.

Collaboration and communication are allies. Collaboration is a tool for the participants to blend their strengths with each other and accomplish a common goal. Good and honest communication facilitates this.

As challenges become more complex, a dedicated entity may find that they are missing vital parts in their solution. Effective collaboration will assess the attributes of the new entities they would like to recruit and see if there are positive ways to blend their assets and offset their liabilities. The success of this will put the collaborative process in motion, where the resultant relationship will create a purpose for all parties to work together for a shared outcome.

Leadership is vital in collaboration. A collaborative leader must exude trust and honesty. Good leaders must be candid, effectively communicate their vision, and treat all members of the collaborative party with respect. The leader's communication includes constant updates on the progress of the project.

A meaningful example of collaboration occurred when our Founding Fathers worked diligently together to form our almost 250-year-old democratic republic. In his book, Founding Brothers, John J.

Ellis captured the importance and effectiveness of collaboration among our Founding Fathers.

Three takeaways from this book that are relevant to the purpose of my book are: (1) The Founding Fathers "had flaws like ordinary citizens," (2) They were "human beings," and (3) They were successful in reconciling their differences to fulfill a "higher purpose."

The 21st century problems cannot be solved by one good citizen alone. It takes several to bond around a common purpose, share and reconcile their differences, and humanly, with the guidance of a higher power, give of themselves to accomplish their collaborative goals.

"None of us, including me, ever do great things.
But we can all do small things, with great love,
and together, we can do something wonderful."

\- Mother Teresa

HUMANISM

A dictionary definition of humanism is: "an outlook or system of thought attaching prime importance to human rather than divine or supernatural matters. Humanist beliefs stress the potential value and goodness of human beings, emphasize common human needs, and seek solely rational ways of solving human problems."

A 2017 blog entitled "Unmasking Humanism" defined humanism this way. "Humanism is a philosophy, worldview, or life stance based on naturalism—the conviction that the universe or nature is all that exists or is real. Humanism serves, for many humanists, some of the psychological and social functions of a religion, but without belief in deities, transcendental entities, miracles, life after death, and the supernatural."

It is evident that our Founding Fathers believed in God. However, they worked collectively and diligently as humans to lay the foundation for the forming of our great country. These were simply good citizens who addressed the roadblocks to their mission using my acronym **ADAPTS**. It is also crystal clear to me that they had **LOVE** and **THE GOLDEN RULE** in their hearts.

As a result, I am not comfortable with humanism solely in a secular way as the vehicle for solving human problems. I opine that belief in a higher power is also required. Therefore, I would prefer to use the term "Spiritual Humanism" as the holistic tool by which good citizens solve major problems.

Spiritual humanism transcends any particular religion and values all spiritual experiences. This philosophy will act to reduce the tribalism that sometimes comes from those who are polarized by their religion being viewed as the only connection to God. By positioning itself outside of religion, spiritual humanism expands the horizons of all. It provides historical knowledge, values the parables of Jesus, and therefore provides the knowledge and wisdom that are key components to problem-solving.

I see it this way. Human beings solve problems. Spirituality works to elevate humans to aspire to be part of something greater than themselves. The major issues of the 21st century require good citizens to seek solutions through a combination of human and spiritual channels.

In her book Humanly Possible, Sara Bakewell quoted Anton Chekhov, who had views of religion and morality that were also humanist. In her book, she wrote that as a nineteenth-century short story writer, playwright, and physician, Anton Chekhov wrote in 1889, in a letter to a friend – alluding to a song by Mikhail Glinka, with words by Alexander Pushkin:

"If man knows the theory of the circulatory system, he is rich. If he learns the history of religion and the song "I remember a Marvelous Moment," in addition, he is the richer, not the poorer, for it. We are consequently dealing entirely on pluses."

Chekhov responded… Dealing in pluses: that is glory enough for me.

Bakewell closes her book on humanism with a creed of Robert G. Ingersoll:

Happiness is the only good.

The time to be happy is now.

The place to be happy is here.

The way to be happy is to make others so.

I, too, believe in the Ingersoll creed. However, I think that a key element to the referenced happiness requires the grounding created by the belief in a higher power. I believe that spiritual humanism was the "special sauce" that was used in Brookhiser's 13.

ADAPTABILITY

When teams work on projects that may require complex strategies and implementing different approaches designed to meet the team's goals, adaptability becomes very important. Adaptive skills, including strategic thinking, effective communication, interpersonal skills, flexibility, and resilience, allow one to teach and learn from others.

Adaptability enables one to adjust from one problem-solving strategy to another when circumstances require it. With today's ever-changing landscape, adaptability becomes a required skill to remain on task. In addition, an adaptable person has the ability to learn new skills if the task at hand requires it.

Because it is impossible to avoid unexpected challenges, having adaptable team members allows for a quicker and more effective recovery from setbacks.

21st-century problems are not solvable unless adaptable leaders step forward, give of themselves, and serve those whom they lead (in the case of Washington's leaders, this should be all Americans) while adapting to the changing challenges of the time.

For example, one of the most critical issues of the 21st century is the attack on our democracy. This concern cannot be quelled unless our leaders adapt to and focus on the causes of the concern. This will take a 360-degree process, which will include our leaders (top-down) responding to our dedicated citizens (bottom-up). This is how it needs to work:

1. Our leaders must accept that there is a problem.

2. Our leaders must adapt to a "new process" in Washington. That is to begin listening to each other without "the outside noise of agitators."

3. Our leaders must re-adapt to their oath to represent all citizens. This includes standing up to those who suffer from the diseases of racism, homophobia, etc.

4. Our leaders must adapt to obvious attempts to destroy our Constitution and radically impede our freedom.

5. Our leaders must adapt and adhere to the value of respect, not only for adversaries but for themselves.

6. Our leaders must adapt to a "new reconstruction" whereby those citizens who are being disenfranchised can retain their rights and have the opportunity to pursue their happiness.

7. Good citizens must adhere to their responsibilities, as I outlined in **REACTION**.

Good citizens are the common denominator to 21st-century solutions such as the attack on our democracy or any of those listed in FACING CHANGE. They have to adapt as well. They need to organize, speak out, and peacefully show our leaders that change is required.

"They demonstrate how motives of bureaucracy are directly opposed to the need for adapting to change. Adaptability is a prime requirement for life to survive."
Frank Herbert, <u>Chapterhouse: Dune</u>

<u>Nobleness</u>

A definition of nobleness is "the quality of elevation of mind and exaltation of character or ideals or conduct." Noble people are considered moral, righteous, ethical, virtuous, and courageous.

Chris McCure described three important qualities of noble leaders in the 2021 article "3 Actions of Noble Leaders." These qualities are: (1) Aspire to greatness, (2) Excel in character, and (3) Do what's right.

Our history includes many figures who demonstrated nobleness, such as George Washington, Abraham Lincoln, Benjamin Franklin, Theodore Roosevelt, Franklin D. Roosevelt, Ronald Reagan, etc. Another relatively current noble leader was Nelson Mandela. Sonia McDonald published a 2022 article entitled "The Top Ten Most Inspirational Leaders Who Led with Courage," where she cited the following synopsis of Mr. Mandela's life.

"Nelson Mandela (1918 – 2013) was a South African anti-apartheid revolutionary, political leader, and philanthropist who served as the first president of South Africa from 1994 to 1999. He was the country's first black head of state and the first elected in a fully representative democratic election. Mandela was instrumental in the formation of the ANC

Youth League, the establishment of the first black law firm in South Africa, and the end of white minority rule in South Africa. He also came out with a host of reforms to support democracy in South Africa.

He helped secure universal suffrage in South Africa and promoted tolerance and reconciliation. Mandela also established a number of charity organizations that allowed him to continue his work in poverty alleviation and social justice. In 1995, he established the Nelson Mandela Children's Fund, which created scholarship opportunities for children across South Africa.

In 1994, Nelson Mandela won the Nobel Peace Prize for his unflinching dedication to peace and social justice in and outside South Africa. He was joint winner with former President F. W. de Klerk."

Mandela definitely possessed the "3 Actions of Noble Leaders." In my mind, the most incredible of Mandela's accomplishments were his reforms to support democracy in the face of white minority leadership.

The qualities of nobleness in our leaders, as well as in their constituents, are required today as we face a drastically changing ethnic landscape. From 1920 to 2020, the white population in the US decreased from 89.7% to 61.6%, while the black population increased from 9.9% to 12.4%. The most significant growth is represented by Asians and Hispanics (1.4% to 24.9%). The remainder of the population today is comprised of Native Americans (approximately 1.2%).

In order to lead with LOVE and THE GOLDEN RULE *(I believe that noble characteristics are included therein)*, these changes in the US population need to be addressed. In many US states, redistricting is occurring that, in many cases, does not result in fairness for all of their ethnic populations. This is a form of disenfranchisement, which blatantly flies in the face of the liberties expected of all citizens as outlined in the Declaration of Independence.

> *"To do good is noble. To tell others to do good is even nobler and much less trouble."*
> **Mark Twain**

<u>Generosity</u>

Generosity is the act of being kind, selfless, and giving to others. Despite being an act that is done to benefit others' well-being, generosity also paradoxically increases our well-being. Generosity can go beyond the individual act and create a culture of generosity. This is much like the "hundredth monkey effect." If many citizens do a good deed, many other citizens will follow.

Bill Hugh, in his article, "Generosity for Impact: Solving the World's Greatest Problems," mentioned the term "mega philanthropist" describing billionaire philanthropists focusing their charitable efforts on solving major problems. According to Hugh, they seek to solve some of the ills in the world, such as artificial intelligence, technical privacy concerns, poverty, and education.

He explains Generosity for Impact as follows:

> Generosity was never meant to be the idea that we land our name on a list because we made a big gift. It was never meant to be the idea of getting our name on a building. Nor should it be a mechanical act—calculating a percentage of income.

> Generosity in its highest and best form is always about meeting needs and solving problems in the world—generosity for impact. In the Christian gospel, Jesus gave his life so that he could save others. The *so that* is critical to generosity.

We need to ask what problems we are solving with our generosity. It may mean funding not just an organization but an idea for solving a problem. Maybe it will mean bringing multiple organizations together to solve a problem.

I know someone who is actively bringing organizations together to solve the larger human trafficking problem.

The beauty of generosity will always be best measured by the impact it's having on the world. It will take grit, persistence, and patience—staying with it for the long haul—to solve those problems.

Generosity designed to solve the world's problems is not just for mega philanthropists. All good citizens can participate. It happens all the time in many ways. My example of giving money to a stranded person and eventually being rewarded with an unrelated gift by the Vietnamese doctor whom I represented in the past is one such instance.

Good citizens have an opportunity today to give to almost any cause. Certain acts of generosity, however, can reach a higher level that will be an example to all. An example is George Washington's voluntary resignation from the Presidency after two terms to demonstrate that our newly formed government does not expect a King-like system of serving for life.

Washington's selfless action needs to be followed today. The 22nd Amendment to the US Constitution limited Presidential terms to two. I don't think we should have stopped there. We probably should have imposed term limits on members of the House of Representatives and the US Senate. Even members of the Supreme Court should be considered for limitations of service, maybe by setting an age limit.

If a US President can only serve a maximum of eight years, I feel that a member of the House shouldn't spend more than four terms (eight years). I further believe that a US Senator should be limited to two terms (12 years). This will make room for more leaders to be involved and allow for their generosity to give to their country.

Federalist 78, written by Alexander Hamilton, argued for lifetime tenure for US Supreme Court Justices. He stated that a lifetime appointment gives Federal Justices (this includes the Supreme Court and other Federal Justices) the ability to work objectively on behalf of the people. He felt that seeking reelection might make them act in bad faith in an effort to retain the office. Hamilton also felt that the only job of the Justice is to review laws to ensure that they abide by the Constitution.

Hamilton made one more very important point in *Federalist 78*. He acknowledges that the laws of the Federal government will quickly become very complicated. Therefore, it will be necessary for a lifetime of study for a person to fit the qualifications needed to serve as a Justice.

This is where I feel Hamilton and other authors of the Federalist Papers failed as it relates to the qualifications and tenure of Supreme Court Justices. The Constitution contains no explicit qualifications for a Supreme Court Justice. No age, education, job experience, or citizenship are required. A Supreme Court Justice doesn't even need a law degree.

If Hamilton believes "a lifetime of study" is required as a qualification, how does he define a lifetime? Is a person 21 years of age, with no law degree or even a college degree, qualified to be a Justice? Also, is the length of Justice's tenure really important for the constitutionality of laws? There have been 16 Supreme Court Justices who have served more than 30 years, including Clarence Thomas. Are they more effective than the 20 who served between 10 and 15 years?

Generosity should also be a characteristic of a Federal Justice who generously applies the law equally to all. I am skeptical that the current system allows for this.

"The greatest gift you can ever give is your honest self."

Fred Rogers

Innovation

What is innovation? In a simple, often-used phrase, it is "out of the box thinking." It is defined as the process of bringing new ideas or solutions that have a major impact or value. It blends ideas and outcomes. It also may require the taking of risks to achieve the desired results. Innovation can lead to small advancements or world-changing outcomes.

One example of innovation that relates to 21st-century solutions is electric vehicles. Tesla has revolutionized the automotive industry by offering long-range capabilities and high-performance features. Rivian has followed with EV solutions for trucks. Almost all existing car companies are following suit. This includes Ford, General Motors, Honda, Toyota, and Hyundai.

By 2050, Wood Mackenzie estimates that 700 million electric vehicles will be on the road. This compares to approximately 16 million today.

I also have some personal examples of innovation that have been relevant to effect positive change. One example was the risk I took during the 2006 Boys & Girls Clubs workshop. I challenged myself to think "out of the box" to find a way to reach my audience and chose my life story as the vehicle. This actually resulted in a new level of teamwork at the organization, resulting in increased productivity.

Another example actually relates to the "hundredth monkey" concept. In 2008, I was Executive Director of the TAG Education Collaborative (TAG Ed). It was the non-profit arm of the Technology Association of Georgia. TAG Eds' mission was to promote the importance of STEM education. This included the development of a program that I am very proud of. It was a summer internship for high school students who were interested in STEM careers in the Metro Atlanta area.

Initially, there was considerable pushback because the high school students were considered too young by many to whom I initially promoted the product. With confidence that it would work, I moved forward. We recruited applicants from several schools along with the technology companies who would fund the program and hire the students for the summer.

This program started slowly but grew each of the three years I was there. We had students performing jobs they would never have dreamed of. One of these internships was for two female high school students who were placed at Georgia Tech's Nanotechnology Center. This was during Georgia Tech's changeover from an outdated center to a brand-new Nanotechnology Research Center funded by Bernie Marcus.

These ladies not only worked on nanotechnology projects but also assisted in the setup of the new facility. Both of these ladies were eventually accepted at Georgia Tech with a Presidential Scholarship. This scholarship was only awarded to a handful of qualified students annually.

Nick Jain of IdeaScale outlined 7 steps in the innovation process. They are as follows.

Step 1. Identify Opportunities

*The first step is to identify opportunities for innovation. This can be done through **market research**, customer insights, trend analysis, or internal assessments. The goal is to uncover unmet needs, emerging trends, or areas for improvement that can be addressed through innovation.*

Step 2. Generate Ideas

*Once opportunities are identified, the next step is to generate ideas. This can be done through brainstorming sessions, idea competitions, **customer feedback**, or cross-functional collaboration. The aim* *is to generate a wide range of creative and innovative ideas that have the potential to address the identified opportunities.*

Step 3. Evaluate and Select Ideas

*After **ideation**, the next step is to evaluate and select the most promising ones. This involves assessing the feasibility, viability, and desirability of each idea. Consider factors such as market potential, technical feasibility, resource requirements, alignment with strategic goals, and potential impact. The goal is to identify the ideas that are worth pursuing further.*

Step 4. Develop and Prototype

Once ideas are selected, they can be further developed and prototyped. This involves translating the selected ideas into tangible prototypes, mock-ups, or minimum viable products (MVPs). The aim is to test and validate the concepts, gather feedback, and refine the ideas based on customer insights and technical feasibility.

Step 5. Test and Iterate

*In this step, the prototypes or MVPs are tested with users or in real-world scenarios. **Customer feedback** is collected, and the concepts are iterated and refined based on the insights gained. This iterative process helps to validate assumptions, uncover potential issues, and improve the innovation before moving to the next stage.*

Step 6. Implement and Scale

Once the innovation has been tested and refined, it can be implemented and scaled up. This involves developing a detailed implementation plan, allocating resources, and executing the necessary actions to bring the innovation to market or implement it within the organization. The goal is to ensure a smooth transition from the development phase to full-scale implementation.

Step 7. Monitor and Evaluate

After implementation, it is important to monitor and evaluate the performance and impact of the innovation. This involves tracking key metrics and performance indicators to assess the success of the innovation. Regular evaluation helps identify areas for improvement, make necessary adjustments, and capture learnings for future innovation initiatives.

*Innovation is an ongoing process, and organizations should foster a **culture of innovation**. This involves capturing feedback, promoting learning from both successes and failures, and continuously seeking new opportunities for innovation. Regularly revisiting and refining the innovation process itself is also essential to optimize the organization's ability to innovate effectively.*

The "out-of-the-box thinking" that results from innovation is critical in solving the complex problems of the 21st century.

"If you want something new, you have to stop doing something old." Peter F. Drucker

<u>Natural Learning</u>

Natural learning generally relates to the type of learning a child receives from homeschooling. Home education pioneer John Holt contended that children have an innate desire to learn and a curiosity that drives them to learn what they need to know when they need to know it. Holt believed that the usual methods of teaching destroy both desire and curiosity. He advocated access to more of the real world, plenty of time and space for their experiences, and opportunities to make meaning out of them.

Holt further stated that natural learners tend to see that knowledge is interrelated rather than compartmentalized. It is also understood that human beings, including children, are intelligent and can generally learn what they choose to learn when they perceive they need to learn it.

The characteristics of natural learning mentioned by Holt carry forward from early education to a lifetime approach to learning. This is what I previously referred to as lifetime learning. Lifetime learning is self-driven and is the responsibility of the learner more so than the teacher. When the learner has a purpose combined with a strong curiosity directed toward a solution to a problem, great things can happen.

Once a good citizen is committed to a life of learning, creative solutions become possible. Colonel Sanders created Kentucky Fried Chicken at age 62. Ray Kroc created McDonald's at age 52. At 54, Benjamin Franklin invented the armonica, which Mozart and Beethoven eventually used.

All of these creators were natural learners who possessed a skill set that included a creative approach to problem-solving, which enabled the end users of their products to have greater enjoyment in their lives.

21st-century problems require natural learners, not necessarily home-schooled students, but lifetime learners committed to effecting change to solve the major problems that we face in the world today and in the future.

"Learning is not attained by chance; it must be sought for with ardour and diligence."
Abigail Adams

Grounded in Values

In order to be able to solve complex and important problems, the problem solver needs to be grounded in ethical values. If this is not the case, the problem solver will be missing an opportunity to see where moral values may be missing in the solution of the problem.

As I mentioned in Chapter 2, effective citizens react in concert with a strong family value system, commitment to learning, adherence to the laws of the land, and respect for and responsibility to

others. My responsibilities as a good citizen (REACTION) are use-
less unless they are grounded in moral values.

An article extracted from the Markkula Center for Applied
Ethics at Santa Clara University provides the following example of a
framework for ethical decision-making.

A Framework for Ethical Decision Making:

Identify the Ethical Issues

1. *Could this decision or situation be damaging to someone or some group
   or unevenly beneficial to people? Does this decision involve a choice between a good and bad alternative, or perhaps between two "goods" or between two "bads"?*

2. *Is this issue about more than solely what is legal or what is most efficient? If so, how?*

Get the Facts

1. *What are the relevant facts of the case? What facts are not known?
   Can I learn more about the situation? Do I know enough to make a
   decision?*

2. *What individuals and groups have an important stake in the outcome? Are the concerns of some of those individuals or groups more
   important? Why?*

3. *What are the options for acting? Have all the relevant persons and
   groups been consulted? Have I identified creative options?*

Evaluate Alternative Actions

1. *Evaluate the options by asking the following questions:*

   - *Which option best respects the rights of all who have a stake?
     (The Rights Lens)*

- *Which option treats people fairly, giving them each what they are due? (The Justice Lens)*

- *Which option will produce the most good and do the least harm for as many stakeholders as possible? (The Utilitarian Lens)*

- *Which option best serves the community as a whole, not just some members? (The Common Good Lens)*

- *Which option leads me to act as the sort of person I want to be? (The Virtue Lens)*

- *Which option appropriately takes into account the relationships, concerns, and feelings of all stakeholders? (The Care Ethics Lens)*

Choose an Option for Action and Test It

1. *After an evaluation using all of these lenses, which option best addresses the situation?*

2. *If I told someone I respect (or a public audience) which option I have chosen, what would they say?*

3. *How can my decision be implemented with the greatest care and attention to the concerns of all stakeholders?*

Implement Your Decision and Reflect on the Outcome

1. *How did my decision turn out, and what have I learned from this specific situation? What (if any) follow-up actions should I take?*

This framework for ethical thinking is the product of dialogue and debate at the Markkula Center for Applied Ethics at Santa Clara University. Primary contributors include Manuel Velasquez, Dennis Moberg, Michael J. Meyer, Thomas Shanks, Margaret R. McLean, David DeCosse, Claire André, Kirk O. Hanson, Irina Raicu, and Jonathan Kwan. It was last revised on November 5, 2021.

As the readers of this book may gain more understanding of how I see the world, they will realize how strongly I see the importance of moral values for effective and lasting problem-solving. The foundation of which is LOVE and THE GOLDEN RULE.

"Each problem that I solved became a rule, which served afterward to solve other problems." **– Rene Descartes**

Failing Forward

Solving problems through failures is a concept often referred to as "failing forward" or "learning from failure." It involves using failures as valuable learning experiences to identify weaknesses, refine strategies, and ultimately achieve success. Here are steps you can take to solve problems through failures:

Embrace a Growth Mindset: Adopt a growth mindset, which means viewing failures as opportunities for growth and learning rather than as setbacks. Recognize that failures are a natural part of the learning and problem-solving process.

Analyze the Failure: When a failure occurs, take the time to analyze it thoroughly. Understand the root causes, what went wrong, and why it happened. This requires honest self-assessment and a willingness to confront mistakes.

Identify Lessons Learned: Extract valuable lessons from failure. What insights can you gain from the experience? What would you do differently next time? Identify specific takeaways that can inform your future actions.

Adjust Your Approach: Use the insights gained from the failure to adjust your approach or strategy. Implement changes that address the weaknesses or mistakes identified during the analysis. Be flexible and willing to adapt.

Set Clear Goals: Reevaluate your goals and objectives in light of the failure. Are they realistic and attainable? Make sure your goals align with your newfound insights and adjusted strategy.

Experiment and Iterate: Don't be discouraged by failure; instead, view it as an opportunity to experiment and iterate. Try new approaches and strategies based on what you've learned. Be open to testing different solutions.

Seek Feedback: Solicit feedback from peers, mentors, or experts in the field. They can provide valuable perspectives and suggestions for improvement. Constructive criticism can be a powerful tool for problem-solving.

Build Resilience: Develop resilience in the face of failure. Understand that setbacks are part of the journey and don't define your overall capability. Stay committed to your goals and maintain a positive attitude.

Document and Reflect: Keep a record of your failures, lessons learned, and the changes you've made. Regularly reflect on your progress and the evolution of your problem-solving approach.

Persist and Iterate: Continue the problem-solving process with persistence. It's common for complex problems to require multiple iterations and adjustments before achieving success. Be patient and keep moving forward.

Share Your Experiences: Consider sharing your experiences and insights with others, especially if you've overcome a significant challenge. Your story of learning from failure can inspire and help others facing similar obstacles.

Remember that not all failures are equal, and some may be more significant or impactful than others. It is essential to differentiate between minor setbacks and major failures that require more in-depth analysis and adjustment. Ultimately, the ability to learn from failures and adapt your approach is a valuable skill for personal and professional growth.

Ambition

Ambition in problem-solving refers to the determination, drive, and willingness to tackle complex challenges and find effective solutions. It involves setting high goals and striving to achieve them through innovative thinking, perseverance, and hard work. Ambitious problem solvers are not content with simple or conventional solutions; they aim to make a significant impact and are willing to push the boundaries of what is possible.

Here are some key characteristics of ambition in problem-solving:

Vision: Ambitious problem solvers have a clear vision of the problem they want to solve and the desired outcome. They can see the bigger picture and set long-term goals.

Persistence: They don't give up easily. Ambitious problem solvers are resilient and continue to work on a problem even when faced with setbacks or obstacles.

Innovation: They are open to trying new approaches, thinking outside the box, and exploring unconventional solutions. They are not afraid to take risks.

Resourcefulness: Ambitious problem solvers are resourceful and can leverage a wide range of tools, information, and expertise to address the issue at hand.

Impact Orientation: They are not satisfied with merely solving a problem; they want their solutions to have a meaningful impact on the world, whether it's improving a process, advancing technology, or making a positive difference in people's lives.

Goal Setting: They set ambitious goals for themselves and their problem-solving efforts. These goals serve as motivation and provide a sense of direction.

Time Management: They effectively manage their time and prioritize tasks to ensure they make progress toward their problem-solving goals.

Ambition in problem-solving can lead to significant achievements and breakthroughs. However, it's essential to balance ambition with practicality and ethical considerations to ensure that the solutions generated are both effective and responsible.

"Our problems are man-made; therefore, they may be solved by man. No problem of human destiny is beyond human beings."
John F. Kennedy

Creativity

Creativity in problem-solving involves thinking in novel and imaginative ways to address challenges, find solutions, and generate innovative ideas. It's a crucial skill in various fields, from business and science to art and everyday life. Creative problem solvers can come up with unique approaches, see connections that others might miss, and adapt to changing circumstances. Here are some key aspects of creativity in problem-solving:

Divergent Thinking: Creative problem solvers often engage in divergent thinking, which means they explore multiple potential solutions or ideas rather than settling for the first one that comes to mind. They generate a wide range of possibilities before narrowing them down.

Unconventional Approaches: They are open to unconventional and non-linear approaches to problem solving. They are willing to challenge existing assumptions and norms.

Combining Ideas: Creativity often involves combining seemingly unrelated ideas, concepts, or elements to create something new and innovative. This can lead to breakthrough solutions.

Flexible Thinking: Creative problem solvers are adaptable and can shift their perspective or approach when faced with unexpected obstacles or new information.

Empathy: Understanding the perspectives and needs of others is crucial for creative problem-solving. Empathy allows problem solvers to design solutions that address real-world issues and improve the lives of individuals or communities.

Inspiration from Different Domains: Creativity often thrives when individuals draw inspiration from diverse fields or sources, bringing fresh insights to their domain.

Iterative Process: Creativity in problem-solving is often an iterative process. Creative individuals are willing to experiment, make mistakes, learn from them, and refine their ideas over time.

Mindfulness and Awareness: Being present and fully engaged in the problem-solving process can help individuals notice subtle details, patterns, or opportunities that might otherwise go unnoticed.

Risk-Taking: Creativity involves a willingness to take calculated risks. Creative problem solvers are not afraid to test unconventional ideas and approaches.

Playfulness: A sense of playfulness and curiosity can stimulate creativity. It encourages individuals to explore, experiment, and have fun while problem-solving.

Visualization: Creative individuals often use visual aids, sketches, diagrams, or other forms of visualization to help conceptualize and communicate their ideas.

Pattern Recognition: Creative problem solvers are adept at recognizing patterns and making connections between seemingly unrelated information, which can lead to innovative insights.

Critical Thinking: Creative problem solving is not just about generating ideas but also critically evaluating and refining them to ensure their feasibility and effectiveness.

Cultivating creativity in problem-solving can be a valuable skill for individuals and organizations looking to tackle complex challenges and find innovative solutions. Encouraging a culture that values and nurtures creativity can lead to more dynamic problem-solving processes and outcomes.

Imagination is more important than knowledge.

Albert Einstein

Expediency

Expediency in problem-solving refers to the ability to address issues or challenges quickly and efficiently, often by making practical and timely decisions. It emphasizes the importance of finding solutions that are both effective and efficient, especially when time is a critical factor. Here are some key aspects and principles of expedient problem-solving:

Prioritization: Identify the most pressing problems or tasks and focus your efforts on resolving them first. Not all problems are equally important, so it's crucial to prioritize based on urgency and impact.

Resource Allocation: Allocate resources such as time, manpower, and budget efficiently. Consider what resources are available and how best to use them to solve the problem as quickly as possible.

Decision-Making: Make decisions promptly but thoughtfully. Sometimes, quick decisions are necessary to prevent a problem from worsening, but it's essential to balance speed with the need for well-informed choices.

Flexibility: Be adaptable in your problem-solving approach. If one solution isn't working, be willing to pivot and try another approach without delay.

Collaboration: Involve others who can contribute to the solution. Working as a team can often lead to quicker problem resolution as individuals can bring different perspectives and expertise to the table.

Lean Thinking: Apply lean principles, such as eliminating waste and unnecessary steps, to streamline processes and make problem-solving more efficient.

Continuous Improvement: After resolving a problem expediently, take the time to analyze what went well and what could be improved for future problem-solving situations. Continuous improvement helps enhance efficiency over time.

Risk Assessment: Assess the risks associated with different solutions. Sometimes, taking a calculated risk can lead to a quicker solution, but it's essential to understand the potential consequences.

Information Gathering: Gather essential information quickly but accurately. In some cases, you may need to make decisions based on limited information, so it's crucial to collect the most relevant data efficiently.

Clear Communication: Communicate your decisions and actions clearly and promptly to all relevant stakeholders. Effective communication helps maintain transparency and ensures everyone is on the same page.

Test and Learn: In situations where you can't immediately implement a complete solution, consider testing more minor changes or solutions to learn from the results and refine your approach iteratively.

Time Management: Manage your time effectively, setting realistic deadlines and milestones for problem-solving tasks. Avoid procrastination and stay focused on the task at hand.

Expediency in problem-solving doesn't mean rushing through decisions without considering their implications. It's about finding a balance between speed and effectiveness, making informed choices, and acting promptly to address the challenges at hand.

There comes a time when one must take the position that is neither safe nor politic nor popular, but he must do it because conscience tells him it is right.

Martin Luther King, Jr.

The CHANGING FACE tools and characteristics of great problem solvers are essential in tackling the problems that face us in the 21st century. These, along with the core values of LOVE and THE GOLDEN RULE, will allow the good citizen to make a difference in the world.

Chapter Eight

Staying on Course

"In the confrontation between the stream and the rock, the stream always wins – not through strength, but through persistence."

– Buddha

"The difference between a successful person and others is not a lack of strength, not a lack of knowledge, but rather a lack of will."

– Vince Lombardi

"Most of the important things in the world have been accomplished by people who have kept on trying when there seemed to be no hope at all."

– Dale Carnegie

The life of a citizen is complex. Like cells in the human body, all citizens are unique and may be unique enough to be a distinct race in itself. Individual citizens grow up in different environments and may have non-traditional family structures. Others sometimes judge their existence based on what they look like or who their friends are. As a result, it is hard to really get to know someone without going beyond the obvious.

As I have already noted, I strongly believe in lifetime learning, which includes an attempt to learn the best in others. This is where my values of LOVE and THE GOLDEN RULE come into play.

My CHANGING FACE approach to problem-solving is important to me because I strongly believe that major problems like the 21st century challenges I described cannot be effectively addressed unless the characteristics of CHANGING FACE are employed.

In my 76 years of living, I have often thought about doing something that makes a difference in the world. Most of these, during a certain period of selfishness, were put aside. Later in my life, I discovered someone brilliant and well-educated, but he spent several years of his early life rebelling and living a sinful life. An association with an honorable mentor put him on track to be one of the greatest Christian figures of all time. This was St. Augustine.

Augustine's early life was characterized by a search for meaning, a quest for knowledge, and a struggle with worldly desires. His eventual conversion to Christianity marked a significant turning point, leading him to become one of the most influential theologians and philosophers in the history of Christianity. His writings continue to be studied and revered by scholars and theologians to this day. His most famous books were Confessions and The City of God.

I was encouraged to read Confessions by a counselor who felt it would make me understand myself better and put me on a path toward understanding my purpose in life. The following is a brief description of the importance of Confessions.

Confessions is a classic work written by Saint Augustine, one of the most influential theologians and philosophers in Christian history. This autobiographical work is not only a reflection on Augustine's personal journey but also a profound exploration of various philosophical, theological, and moral themes. Here are some of the key lessons and insights that can be learned from the book Confessions:

The Nature of Sin and Redemption: Augustine's Confessions is deeply introspective, and he candidly reflects on his early life, including his sinful actions and wayward behavior. Through his own experiences, he emphasizes the universality of sin and the need for redemption and forgiveness through Christ.

The Power of Self-Examination: Augustine's process of self-examination and self-awareness is central to Confessions. He encourages readers to engage in introspection to examine their own lives, actions, and motivations critically. This introspection can lead to personal growth and a deeper understanding of one's relationship with God.

The Role of Divine Grace: Augustine's conversion is a central theme in Confessions. He attributes his transformation from a life of worldly pursuits to a life devoted to God to the intervention of divine grace. This underscores the Christian belief in the transformative power of God's grace and the capacity for individuals to change their lives through faith.

The Pursuit of Wisdom and Truth: Augustine's intellectual journey is another significant aspect of the book. He sought wisdom and truth through various philosophical and religious traditions, including Manichaeism and Neoplatonism, before ultimately finding them in Christianity. His quest for intellectual and spiritual fulfillment serves as an example of the human thirst for knowledge and meaning.

The Role of Memory: Augustine delves into the concept of memory, exploring how memories shape our identities and influence our actions. He suggests that memory can be a powerful tool for spiritual reflection and personal growth, as it allows us to recall our past experiences and learn from them.

The Love of God: Throughout Confessions, Augustine expresses his deep love for God. His fervent desire for God's presence and his longing for a profound union with the divine serve as a powerful example of Christian devotion.

The Importance of Storytelling and Confession: Confessions itself is a form of confession and storytelling. Augustine's willingness to share his struggles, doubts, and spiritual journey is a testament to the power of confession and narrative in the process of healing and redemption. Confessions is not only a historical document but also a timeless work that continues to inspire readers to reflect on their own lives, seek spiritual truth, and strive for a deeper connection with God. Its themes and insights have made it a foundational text in Christian theology and literature.

This book allowed me (at age 45) to take a hard look at myself and ask a few questions of myself, such as (1) Who am I? (2) What is my purpose for the rest of my life? (3) Am I living up to the expectations that my wife and kids have for me? (4) Am I a benefit or bad influence on the lives of my friends?

St. Augustine's work, City of God, further influenced my life. In this work, Augustine introduces the central theme of the book: the distinction between the "City of God" and the "City of Man." The City of God represents the heavenly city where God's love and eternal salvation reign. The City of Man symbolizes the earthly city, characterized by sin, corruption, and temporal concerns.

City of God is a complex and comprehensive work that engages with numerous theological, philosophical, and historical themes. Augustine's ideas continue to influence Christian thought and provide valuable insights into the relationship between Christianity and the world.

I read this book shortly after I read Confessions. The two books together allowed me to think about life in a different, more inclusive way. I now feel that it is possible to merge my life in the City of Man with the spiritual life in the City of God.

Once I started drinking when I was 18 until age 45, my life had been all about me. I didn't want to, but I made everyone in my life second to me, including God. I knew a major change was required. I had already begun treatment for alcohol abuse, and the second step to recovery was in my mind. That is, "Came to believe that a Power greater than ourselves could restore us to sanity."

Was I crazy? I asked myself. Then, it occurred to me that the guiding principles in the 12 steps to recovery used by Alcoholics Anonymous were really all about spiritual growth. I felt like Mama Kitty's switch had hit me. I now became aware that I had to get closer to God for me and those around me.

I was baptized into the Baptist church when I was very young. Early in this program, I did get a basic understanding of right and wrong. Over time, however, I didn't allow religion to connect me with God better. So now, after many poor decisions in my life, I decided to convert to Catholicism. This was important to me because my wife's family and my children were baptized as Catholics.

It must be said that I am not a perfect Catholic. In addition, I believe that followers of all religions have the potential connection to a higher power that has the capacity to provide them comfort and ground them into a life of good citizens.

My life as a Catholic or, better said for me, my life as a believer in God to guide me through my life journey has connected me to a better sense of doing the right thing. AA and the Catholic church facilitated this awareness.

I have been retired for almost ten years now. During the first part of my retirement, I spent more time with my family. However, I also spent a lot of time at coffee clutches with a group of people who basically didn't really listen to each other unless they agreed on something. Sports was actually our major topic of conversation. After a few years, I realized I needed something more.

I knew that two things interested me: (1) kids and (2) senior citizens. I had already spent 20 years in non-profit programs that benefited kids, so I turned my attention to senior citizens.

Early in 2018, I volunteered at an upscale senior living facility to assist the Director of Activities. As time went on, I was allowed to carve out my niche. I conducted a weekly session called Current Events and presented historical facts that led to a discussion on the events of the day. I was also allowed to conduct a trivia session, assist with bingo, introduce poker, and play bridge with some of the residents.

When COVID-19 hit in 2020, I gravitated away from these weekly meetings. Eventually, however, I did introduce a weekly Zoom meeting with some to continue our discussion on current events.

I have developed some wonderful friendships during my time at the center, which includes a couple who my wife and I see frequently for breakfast. The husband of that couple has become a regular bridge partner of mine. We play online a couple of times a week.

I have probably not made much of a difference in solving any of the major issues referred to in Chapter 6. But I feel comfortable that I have used many of the characteristics required to make a difference. I have done this in small ways. In some cases, it is just being generous, adapting to change, active listening, or a strong commitment to learning. In some cases, it is my collaboration with experts in a certain field and with friends who are morally grounded.

As a result, as I continue to grow and introduce others to the elements of my growth, I have the hope that I will be able to reach others who may have the ability to solve the serious problems that are facing the world today.

My journey toward good citizenship has been filled with good and bad. All of which brought me to where I am today. I am finally at peace.

Cultivate the habit of being grateful for every good thing that comes to you and to give thanks continuously. And because all things have contributed to your advancement, you should include all things in your gratitude.

Ralph Waldo Emerson